STOP PROCRASTINATING:

67 Proven Tactics to Beat Procrastination for Good

*Get Things Done and Stop Your Bad Habits,
Little-Known Life Hacks to Boost Your
Productivity + Step-by-Step 30-Day Plan*

Table of Contents

INTRODUCTION

Success and failure in life can be traced to one nurtured habit or the other. The things that make up your daily activities, the little mechanisms upon which your life runs, will ultimately determine how much you end up achieving. Habits build up into a daily routine, and these routines run our lives. All of these habits have been formed over time, through constant and dedicated practice. In this modern age, procrastination has become embedded into our DNA. The habit of procrastination has robbed most people of overwhelming success in life while enticing them with short-term feel-good rewards for just living the moment. Procrastination is a dream killer; a slow poison that dries up your zeal to achieve and leaves you wallowing in mediocrity. Procrastination is every promise you made to yourself but ended up breaking. Procrastination is when you let the goals you have slide due to lack of motivation. Procrastination is the roadblock that hindered you from reaching the place you had envisioned to be in five years ago.

Procrastination, even in its simplicity, is complex. Don't be deceived. In this book, I am going to unpack and dismantle the concept of procrastination. To enable you to tackle procrastination, you will need to understand the mechanism on which it works. Once the mechanism is fully understood, then techniques can be put in place to disrupt the mechanism. Throughout the chapters of this book, I will reveal to you various tricks and tactics used by the most productive people to overcome procrastination. I will be teaching you how to make good use of your willpower and stay motivated throughout the process. I only need you to believe that procrastination can be conquered and you will see yourself working to overcome it.

I am a self-help instructor with over five years of experience in helping people overcome the greatest hindrances to success. Through the years, I've noticed that the most subtle and dangerous obstacle has been procrastination. Clients walk up to me and complain about how they have put all success habits in place but have not achieved success. They seem to forget the place of time, which is a very crucial ingredient to success. Preparing for an exam a month before and two days before will not produce the same results. The reason for the latter is primarily due to a procrastinating mindset. This is why I decided to write the book to help people identify the bugs of procrastination clogging their lifestyle.

Now! Only a few people understand the power of that single word. Now encapsulates the present, the process of maximizing today. Everyday opportunities present themselves in deceptive manners. Some are quickly identified, and others would take the third eye to catch. However, catching these opportunities is one thing, maximizing them in that same instant they are found is another. Once procrastination is subdued, you instantly begin to reap the benefits in the now. Getting rid of procrastination is simply getting rid of weights that hold you back from acting when you know you should take action. Every opportunity seeping past you or ideas dangling in your head is tied to a deadline. Once the deadline is missed, the overwhelming success attached to that opportunity has been forfeited. And sometimes we won't ever come across such opportunities ever again. I am sure that sounds like that has once happened to you. Don't worry. You will learn to conquer it soon.

Each new day for me comes with a fresh testimony from somebody who has taken time to listen and apply some of the techniques I put into their hand. I receive calls from time to time from people who are glad they attended one seminar or another that I have given in the past. Their testimonies are wide-ranging and vast, covering a range of professions that had once proven to be stagnant before they were revived with the techniques I have been teaching. I discovered that the testimonies are somehow becoming overwhelming, and the testifiers were pressuring me to deliver more and more of my techniques. That is where the vision for this book came along. My main aim was to document as much as I could in one compilation so that these principles can go to places I might never be able to reach and continue the wonders they have been performing.

I have written this book in a simple style to so as not to alienate any of my readers. The techniques will be presented to you, the reader, in such a way that they can be easily followed and practiced. There are dozens of other titles out there that will only criticize you for procrastinating but will never provide you with enough information to counter your procrastination problem. There are little things that can be identified and worked on to give you the best experience while pursuing your goals. Did you know that a factor as negligible as dieting can affect how much you procrastinate? Of course, you will never hear that anywhere else. Just stick with me for this experience.

Some people have spent years procrastinating on the action to stop themselves from procrastination. In essence, they are just procrastinating on a miracle in their lives, the change that could take them to the next level. The great author, Paulo Coelho, said, "One day you will wake, and there won't be any more time to do the things you have always wanted to do. Do it now!" The subject of death is a sacred and greatly feared topic, yet it is so important. That said, you should keep in mind that every single day is drawing you closer to your death. If you don't start to change your life right now and get rid of procrastination, you will soon look back and have a trail of regrets following behind you.

I have heard people say that ideas rule the world. I beg to differ. In my opinion, it is ideas with the corresponding action that rules the world. Any life devoid of action is a life devoid of results, and what is a life worth living when there are no results to show for? Nothing in this book will be worth reading if you are not ready to apply the laid down principles that will be dished out to you. Your mind will continue to trick you into procrastinating on the change process, but it is up to you to conquer those mental roadblocks and take action. I will be stocking your arsenal with the weapons needed to bring down the enemy holding you back from reaching your full potential.

CHAPTER ONE: BEATING LAZINESS

Laziness can go by different names at different times. Some refer to it as slothfulness, others call it idleness or a lackadaisical state of mind. But whatever the name is, we can all agree that laziness in any form is an undesirable trait that can rob you of success. Laziness is a state of mind, a psychological problem. You can refer to laziness as the unwillingness to use up stored energy. Or it can be said to be an unwillingness to undertake a task that you feel is difficult, boring, or time-consuming. Naturally human is laziness, and it takes an extra effort to overcome this innate nature and actually get things done. It is naturally easier to lie down all day long and get nothing done, to forfeit your goals and just watch time rush by. It seems like we humans are simply conditioned to live in mediocrity, to stay comfortable with anything that doesn't challenge our existence or survival. And this is the root of laziness, the foundation on which procrastination exists.

From a young age, the human body has always been bent on instant gratification. But truth be told, your dreams and aspirations will take time before they come to fruition. Allowing laziness become the order of the day will have you watching the seeds you have planted over time dry up before your face. Relating this to our present age, we seek people who absolutely live for nothing. Nothing inspires them, moves them to achieve more, or to do more to change their world. We see people who have accepted life simply for what it is. Technological advancements and changes in society has helped to facilitate the "Laziness Cause" even further. We now exist in a world where you can stay home all day and have everything brought to your doorsteps—your meals, your laundry, your groceries, etc. So, the question remains, "Why work, when everything can be done for you?"

Laziness and Your Goals

Of course, you can get comfortable with laziness and live the rest of your life bothering about nothing. Fact is, you will end up in mediocrity and with no tangible achievements to boast about. But if you are the kind of person that actually lives for something, that has a plan to outgrow their present level and become a success story that family and friends will want to identify with, then laziness is not an option.

One reason people are not motivated to work is that they can't see the beauty behind the achievement of long-term goals. Your laziness exists simply because you are uncomfortable with your present state. Once you make up your mind to leave your present state and enter the next phase of life, laziness begins to shake in its boots knowing that it is about to be knocked off. That is what you should do now. Don't procrastinate the elimination of laziness from your life. The more you postpone the action you need to take, the longer it takes before your dream come to fulfillment.

7 TACTICS TO BEAT LAZINESS

Nobody likes being lazy. That is a funny truth. Most people who have discovered traits of laziness in their everyday life are not fully about the situation. The painful part is that figuring out what to do about laziness is hard. Think about your life at the moment: What are those things you would love to improve upon, ranging from family relationships, career prospects or financial status? All of these things are achievable; they can be improved upon to produce enviable results. There are tactics that can be implemented to help you overcome laziness in this regard and come out with overwhelming success. Let's study some of them:

1. **Have a clearly-defined strategy**

Laziness can't even be overcome if you haven't put down a strategy to go about achieving a particular goal. Say you want to get out of bed in the morning and achieve something for the day. You will need to have a list of actions set up for the day to help you identify where you should start with. In fact, having a well-structured strategy is already halfway to defeating laziness. The important question here will be: What is it that I want and how am I going to do it? Have a brainstorm session and identify ways of achieving your goals. Where do you need to go? Who do you need to talk to? How are you going to do one thing or the other? Write them down from the beginning of the process to the end. One thing you will notice as you put down your plans is that the joy of seeing them accomplished will come over you. That a step in the right direction.

2. **Be self-aware**

Laziness is a stealthy beast. You need know when it is around. Or maybe you know but you just can't do anything about it. One way to tackle laziness is the ability to identify what your laziness is. Laziness for you might be sitting through hundreds of Netflix movies all day and getting nothing done, but that is not laziness for a movie analyst or critic who gets paid to watch and rate movies. Other people can spend hours in a bathtub filled with bubbles and sipping red wine from a wine glass. That can be seen as relaxation, but at some point, it becomes outright laziness. Know how to identify when your relaxation has gradually slipped into laziness. Once you have been able to identify the presence of laziness, then it will be easier for you to fight it.

3. **Learn to love the things you do**

If you dislike an activity, the urge to do it will forever be missing. Sometimes, people aren't lazy, but they are not motivated to perform a certain task, and that results in "laziness." There are straight-A students who will procrastinate on writing their English essays because they hate writing, but they can spend hours and hours in calculus operations. Now these students not necessarily lazy, but writing essays is not something they enjoy. Although they might end up producing wonderful essays, the motivation to start was lacking, and this caused them to procrastinate.

Learning to appreciate whatever you need to do is a skill that needs to be developed over time. It might be a slow or gradual process, but in the end, it will surely pay off. Acquiring the right mindset will definitely have a drastic effect on how much you get done.

4.   Set a timeframe

It could range from 10 minutes to one hour, and in this period tell yourself that there will be no break until you have carried out that task. You have thesis work to type? Sit behind your computer and type for the next ten minutes and see how far you can go with that. Set an alarm to gauge how much you can get done within that timeframe. Usually, your mind will immediately be conditioned to keep going after that task. In fact, your mind might become excited about the next challenge, seeing how much it has been able to accomplish within ten minutes. Once you get involved with the process, it is quite tempting to stop. After conquering the 10-minute challenge, you can then go further and keep pushing yourself. Go for a 30-minute benchmark and see how you fare. Then go for an hour, and so on. But remember that discipline is the key here. If you are failing at staying put for 10 minutes, there is a good chance that you will not succeed at 30 minutes. So, before you go any further, ensure that your body now understands what it means to sit and work for 10 minutes.

5.   Shut down any escape route for the time being

What are those things that can constitute distractions for you and cause you to get lazy and procrastinate? Ask yourself: Where do I always escape to whenever I am not willing to work? Could it be a book, or a video game, or even Instagram? Whatever it is, it should be removed and taken far from you. Uninstall those apps if need be. Lock up those game pads in a drawer if need be. Do these things until you have achieved something worth achieving.

6.   Scold yourself

When there is no one else to check on your excesses, you have to do that for yourself. When you no longer stay with your parents or someone older than you who can shout you out of bed, you should be able to do that for yourself. Remember that your body and mind are built to serve you, and they become quite dormant when allowed to do so. Get strict with your own self. You might call it discipline, but that word has been overused and has little value. Give yourself a talking to and say the things that you are scared to tell your own self. That way, your mind will understand that you aren't playing around anymore.

7.   See the benefits

There is always something in store for you whenever you perform a task. Identify these benefits and brood over them. Take some time to appreciate them and see a future where they have all been accomplished successfully. Imagine the adventures you could possibly encounter by just beating laziness and taking that first step. Of course, there will be difficulties, obstacles and the like, but don't fixate on those. They will only discourage and help ruin the moment.

10 ESSENTIAL ENERGY-BOOSTING FOODS

A lot of people notice that they easily get tired, even after performing small activities at some point during the day. We have all been there at one point or another. It's 12 PM and you already notice that you can't drag your body off a chair. Your body suddenly become heavier. Taking in just any kind of food during this time does not help the situation. Keep in mind that food items that are high in fat and calories will leave you more fatigued than you were before eating them. They usually require more energy to digest.

Lack of energy can drastically affect your performance and your willingness to work. The truth is that the quantity and quality of food you eat can greatly affect your energy levels throughout the day. There are a variety of foods that are known to give energy, but only a handful of these contain the essential nutrients needed to increase the energy levels and keep you alert throughout the day. Foods like sugar or refined carbs can give quick jolts of energy that die within hours. But the body needs energy that is more sustainable, and this can only come from a well-planned diet. Work these following examples into your meals and see the wonder they will work in helping you combat laziness.

1.   Brown Rice

This not the first food that might come to mind as per energy provision, but brown rice does wonders. Unlike white rice, brown rice is less processed and retains more nutritional value in the form of fiber. Brown rice is very rich in manganese, and it converts protein and carbs into fuel to energize the brain and body. This food released energy slowly and steadily throughout the day, helping to keep you motivated and alert. Brown rice can be served with vegetables to enhance its energy provision function.

2.   Sweet Potatoes

Apart from their almost sugary taste, sweet potatoes are also very good energy boosters. They are very high in carbohydrates, beta-carotene (Vitamin A) and vitamin C which will keep fatigue at bay throughout the day. A small-sized sweet potato could contain about 22 grams of carbohydrates, 28% of the RDI (Reference Daily Intake) for manganese and an impressive 438% of the RDI for Vitamin A. The body digests sweet potatoes at a very slow pace thereby providing you with a steady supply of energy. Sweet potatoes can either be fried or boiled and taken with tomato sauce.

3.   Bananas

Bananas are composed mostly of sugars such as glucose, fructose and sucrose. They also have some quantity of fiber in them. Bananas are a very good source of carbohydrates, potassium and vitamin B6, all known to provide the body with steady energy. Have a banana with peanut for a well-rounded snack, or throw slices of them into your morning cereal and watch yourself stay energized throughout the day.

4.   Honey

A spoonful of honey is as powerful as half a cup full of energy drink. Honey usually acts as a time-released muscle fuel during exercise and it helps to replenish muscles after a workout session.

5.   Eggs

A single egg contains about 70 calories in all, plus another 6 grams of proteins. Leucine, an amino acid present in eggs, helps cells take in more blood sugar, stimulate the production of energy in the cells and increase the breakdown of fat to produce energy. The energy released from an egg meal is provided very slowly for the body to utilize. Eggs are also very rich in B vitamins that help enzymes perform their roles in the food breakdown process. Eggs are also known to contain more nutrients in one calorie than most other foods. These nutrients can help to keep the hunger away for a long period of time. You can have your eggs scrambled, boiled, fried, or as an omelet.

6.   Beans

Beans are very high in protein, and conventionally proteins are not believed to provide energy. But that is a wrong belief. Beans are a great source of energy, especially if you are a vegetarian. It contains a lot of fiber which slows down digestion. It is also rich in magnesium that directly supplies your cells with energy.

7. Coffee

Coffee provides you with that early morning jolt needed to get you alert and prepared for the day's activities. It works, and that is why a lot of people have a cup of coffee every morning to start their day. Coffee is high in caffeine which passes quickly from your bloodstream over to your brain where it inhibits the activity of adenosine, a neurotransmitter that quiets the central nervous system. But it should not be abused. When taken in excess, it can get you jittery and interfere with your sleep.

8. Dark Chocolate

This one rings strange, right? Let me explain. Dark chocolate contains more cocoa content than normal milk chocolate or any other form of chocolate. It contains antioxidants that assist in blood flow around the body thereby aiding the spread of energy. Because of this, oxygen is delivered more effectively to the brain and muscles. Also, the increased blood flow caused by these antioxidants also helps to reduce mental fatigue and help the mood.

9. Avocados

They are highly rich in healthy fats and fiber. The fats help to facilitate blood fat levels and encourage the absorption of nutrients from the bloodstream. They are also stored up in the body and used up for energy when it is necessary. The fiber in avocados, which accounts for about 80% of the whole content, can help to maintain steady energy flow around the body. Avocados also contain a lot of B Vitamins which are required if the cell mitochondria will perform optimally.

10. Nuts

Walnuts and almonds are noted to contain enough omega-3 and omega-6 fatty acids, and antioxidants which can increase energy levels and distribution in the bloodstream. Nuts have high calories, proteins, carbs and fats. All of these are nutrients that nuts release slowly throughout the day keeping you energized. Vitamins and minerals such as manganese, iron and vitamin E are some of the treasures that can be found in nuts. All of these give little jolts of energy in their own small ways.

5 TRICKS TO GET ENERGIZED AND STAY ENERGIZED

Staying energized throughout the day is one sure way to get hold of laziness and prevent procrastination. The energy that is referred to here can be mental energy, physical energy or psychological energy. A deficiency in any of the following of them can cause a slowdown of the other bodily process. In our world today, it is commonplace to find out that you have totally become zapped of energy and you have lost your zest for life. Nothing breeds procrastination more than that. If you discover that you suddenly lack energy to carry on, then there are a lot of tricks you can use to snap out of it.

1.   **Do something fun**

This one can help you deal with mental stress. The brain is a fun-loving sense organ that hates monotony and boredom. Once you have kept on with one task for so long and the brain gets tired performing the task, the zeal to return to it a second time and perform that task will never be there. Because the brain will dread that moment. Pause for a while and get your brain to do something different. Pick up your cat and stroke its fur. Play a little hide-and-seek with the dog. Listen to music while you work. Make sure you add a little fun to whatever it is you are doing, but you will want to make sure that you don't become distracted. After some time, you should get back to work.

2.   Take a short power nap

Avoid the temptation to keep working and ignore the tiredness and stress. You are not a machine, and even machines themselves rest. Once you feel drowsiness coming over you, take out a few minutes and have some sleep. You can just bow your head on your table replenish your mind and alertness. If only you can understand the wonder of a short nap. It is like rebooting a system. Everything comes out new and refreshed, ready for a new phase.

3.   Go outside

Get some sunlight and fresh air. Your body itself is always yearning for a new environment from time to time. If you have been in an office with air conditioning for hours at a time, it is time for you to go breathe some fresh air somewhere more natural. Walk to a park and watch the scenery. Observe the children playing with their pets and smile a little. Who knows, you might get inspired for next art project.

4.   Play mind games

Get your brain and mind to work. Their dormancy might be the reason for your lack of energy. Do something that will challenge your mind, brain, and thought patterns. Read an article from the internet or a short story from a book. Play chess with your computer. Brainstorm with your colleagues. All of these things get your brain going and your body will instantly follow suit.

5.   Reduce your workload

One major reason for fatigue and energy loss is size of workload. With a large workload you either get plenty things done badly or you get only a few done correctly. Streamline your daily activities so that stress can be controlled. Pay more attention to the most important activities. Then consider getting help from if you feel it is necessary.

CHAPTER TWO: POWERING UP PRODUCTIVITY

Productivity is the direct opposite of laziness. Once laziness has been successfully conquered, productivity comes next. Productivity requires a step-by-step approach for it to be achieved. It isn't just a one-off activity. That is why it is necessary to put systems in place to get things done when they should be done. This system will define your way of doing things, your methods, and processes. These systems can be developed, or they can be learned. In this chapter, I am going to reveal to you some systems that can help you get things done and become more productive.

GETTING THINGS DONE (GTD)

GTD is an effective way to organize and track your tasks and projects. The main aim of the GTD method of productivity is to ensure a 100% trust in a system for collecting tasks and ideas and plans. The GTD provides you with a way to track what you need to do per time and how you need to do it. Once the GTD system is in place, the amount of stress that you will go through trying to remember all the things that should be continuously done will be greatly reduced. Time is also saved in the long run. The GTD works by keeping lists with a paper and a pen. The main lists you will have to make with the GTD method include:

1. In

The In list contains all of your main ideas and action points as they occur to you. Just jot them down as they come to you and ensure that you miss not a single thing. You can use a notepad and a pen for this or an app on your phone. Just go with whatever works for you. What is important is that you miss nothing as they come.

2. Next Action

This list contains all of the possible actions you may want to take in the near future. From this list, you will pick out what you will need to do next when you are less busy.

3. Waiting For

The items on this list are those that have you anticipating for something to happen. Let's say you have assigned a task to someone and awaiting their reply. The waiting list is the perfect list to put that down. Write that down with a current date so you can keep track of the person's progress.

4. Projects

A project in this regard refers to any task that requires more than one action to get it done. All of these tasks should fall into your project lists. You can make it more interesting by writing down the details of each project so that it can be used as a guide.

On top of these lists, you might need a small calendar to keep track of time-sensitive tasks and events.

ZEN TO DONE METHOD (ZTD)

The Zen to Done method was specifically developed by productivity strategist Leo Babauta to help individuals build habits in a step by step manner while working through a workflow management system. The ZTD teaches one to form one positive habit after another. It makes the whole process a lot easier when these things are tackled in this manner. Some people have found out that they perform better using the ZTD method over the GTD method. The key here is to find which of them works best for you. There are ten habits that should be adopted one at a time over the course of thirty days. Experiment with them until you notice changes in your habit pattern.

1. **Collect**

   Record your ideas into a book or a notepad. Write down ay tasks, ideas, or projects that may come to your mind at any point in time. This is different from the GTD style because the ZTD mandates you to carry a simpler tool such as a notebook or a stack of cards, which are easier to carry about.

2. **Process**

   Don't allow things to pile up and fuel your procrastination. Process your email, voicemails, etc. Put a decision on all of those items as you work: delete, delegate, file it, or do it later.

3. **Plan**

   Set out the things you wish to achieve each week. Ensure that each day is a step forward towards achieving that big project for the week. Be sure to achieve something daily.

4. **Do**

   Eliminate all distractions and get to it. Declutter your work desk and your mind so that you can have even more focus. With the distraction out of the way, set a timer and focus on the task for as long as possible. Don't try to multitask.

5. **Use streamlined lists and tools**

   Keep your lists as simple as possible. Don't allow the tools used in ZTD distract you from achieving productivity. Don't get caught struggling with the tools. Soon, you might find that the system has become too complicated for you to go on with it.

6. **Stay organized**

   Everything that belongs to you must belong to a space in your home. Once you are done using an item, it should be returned to that space. Create an organized system that works and helps you keep track of your items. Treat the organization habit like any other habit that should be developed and work towards developing it. Within 30 days there will be splendid results.

7. **Do a weekly review**

   Select a few of the long-term goals that you would love to focus on and accomplish with a space of six months to one year. Choosing many goals will only leave you overwhelmed without any tangible success. Break down a long-term goal into medium-term goals that will take a shorter time to accomplish. Create short-term weekly goals for each of these other goals. Each week, make a review of how far you have come in accomplishing that short-term goal during the week.

8. **Simplify**

   Your goals should be reduced to the essentials. Do a short review of all of your tasks and projects and find if you can simplify them. Even as you simply them, make sure that they align to the ultimate yearly goals so that you don't find yourself derailing slowly. Select only the stuff that matter.

9. **Set a routine and follow it**

   Build and develop routines that matter. Some these can include meditating, going for a walk each morning or reading at least a page each day. These routines can be developed for different times of the day, be it evening, morning, or afternoon. Also, develop a daily routine for different days of the week.

10. **Run with your passion**

This last one is very important. If you are passionate about your work, the urge to procrastinate doing them will be greatly reduced or quenched totally. Constantly seek things that you are passionate about and pursue them for the greater good. If possible, make a career out of practicing them. Having such a list will give you the fulfillment that you crave as you accomplish each of those tasks and projects.

8 PRODUCTIVITY APPS YOU NEED IN YOUR LIFE RIGHT NOW

A productivity app is a software that makes your job easier and helps you gets things done in lesser. With the help of faster processors and wider connectivity, our smartphones have become some form of personal assistants to us. If you are aiming to improve your productivity level, some of the apps listed below should be at the top of your list. Each year, more and more of these apps are released, providing new and improved ways of staying on track of activities. Here are some of the essential apps that can boost productivity.

1. ToDoList

This app has been downloaded more than 7 million times from various app store platforms. All you need to do is pen down everything you need that you need to get done, and the app goes ahead to interpret and categorize all of your tasks based on the entries. The apps help you and your team stay on track while planning projects, discussing the details, and monitoring deadlines. The app goes for $36 per year for a premium version and $60 a year for full access to your entire team.

2. TeamViewer

This amazing app allows you access to all of your remote devices no matter where you are viewing them from. You can be in one place, and the app instantly connects to the files you need that is currently located somewhere else. The connection also goes as far as giving you the leverage to hold audio meetings, video chats, and file-sharing options. With all of these features, collaboration with a wider variety of people becomes easier, and things get done faster. The app is available for iOS users and Android users.

3. Yelling Mom

Yelling Mom is a fun app to use. It works on the principles of a nagging mother who won't allow you breathing space until you have done what she told you to do. Once you schedule a task, the app goes to remind you about the task before the deadline is over by making use of some annoying alerts like a wailing siren or a referee's whistle.

4. Serene

Serene is designed specifically to handle distractions and help you give more concentration to the things that need to be achieved for that day. The app is currently in a private beta stage, and you will need an invite to be able to use it. But it is worth keeping an eye on for the meantime.

Once you have set up your goal for the day, you will be required to break them down into smaller sessions which will last about 30 to 60 minutes each. Set a timeframe that will be long enough to complete the goal. Once a session starts, the app blocks out any app that might turn out to be a distraction. A countdown appears on the screen while you work, and there is an option to play soothing music as you work.

5. Coach.me

Coach.me is a platform that connects you with online coaches who will help you achieve your goals. You will find different coaches who are specialists in different categories you can choose from. The coaching is done by email, and it is beautiful because you get to meet somebody and make a friend as you change your habits. The coaches will reply to any questions you have.

6. Loop

Loop is an Android-only app, and it employs a rather different approach to helping you concentrate on tasks. Loop is a habit-building app. Instead of getting you away from bad habits, it helps you form new and beneficial ones. Whatever it is that you should invest more time doing, Loop will help you to do it. The major features of this app include

- setting a target for things that you invest more time doing
- Provide a score for how well you are performing in developing new habits
- Set reminders to energize you when laziness sets in

7. HelloSign

HelloSign takes away the trouble involved in signing a large number of documents by giving an option to sign them electronically. All documents that are signed through this app are legally binding because the signature remains real and not electronically engineered. An extra benefit is that all documents signed through the app are all organized so that you don't have to waste time sorting through them whenever you may need them.

8. Drafts

Note-taking and journaling just became easier with the Drafts app. Once a new entry is made, the app quickly tags them and sorts them out. You can use some of the tools in the app to convert your notes to emails, tweets, emails, or documents.

12 MORNING ROUTINE HABITS FOR PRODUCTIVITY

A good morning always results in a good day. And your morning routine seems to really be a major factor that sets the tone for the rest of the day. The success of your day is dependent on the very little details of your morning. You have to understand yourself and the way in which your body works to be able to grasp the full potential of your morning routine fully.

Morning routines have been proven to help some of the most successful people on the planet to achieve their goals. Once productivity is missed in the morning, it is always hard to capture at any other point during the day. Here, we will study some simple morning routine that will help you boost your productivity during the day.

1. Wake up naturally

For one person, 4 AM the perfect time to wake up and start up the day. For another person, a perfect day starts up at 6 AM. The 6 AM person isn't necessarily for waking up some hours later. Take your time to get up from the bed. I am not preaching laziness here, but there are some times that the body itself still needs to gather itself out of bed. Forcing out of bed is one sure way to create chaos. The most important thing is to get your body in tune. Some people function better during nighttime, and they end getting up late from the bed. They have been productive for that day at least. Only make sure that your body stays alert when it is time for it to produce. Resting your mind and brain long in bed is better than staying out of bed and nodding off throughout the process. You will get nothing done right that way.

2. Don't make major decisions in the morning

It is better that you spend the evening before writing down ideas and preparing for the next day. The willpower to make good choices and decisions is greatly reduced in the morning, and it can slow down your brain from performing at an optimum level. Once you have your day all planned out form the night before, it will help your mind to immediately get settled and get to work on the day's activities.

3. Start your day with exercise

You might have heard this about a thousand times, but the importance of exercise to your body cannot be overemphasized. Your body is begging you to train it and let off some steam. People who exercise first thing during a workday are generally known to possess more energy for the day than others. You don't have to visit a gym. You can walk to the train station, skip a hundred times, or do something else that stretches your body.

4. Clean and declutter your workspace

An uncluttered workspace will give you more concentration and productivity. Once everything is disorganized, your ability to perform optimally is reduced. People who work in a clean and organized environment are generally more productive than others who are comfortable with clutter. Clutter takes your time because your work items will be easily misplaced.

5. Complete the hardest and most tedious tasks in the morning

One beautiful thing about the morning is that your mind is as clear as possible. Your internal environment is serene and ready to perform for the day. You should prioritize this opportunity and get things down, especially those things that matter to you. Settle all of those things before your emails start jumping in, and the calls start coming. Once you clear off those tasks, the rest of the day will go on more smoothly.

6. Have a glass of cold water

Hydration helps to bring your body alive. For the whole of the time you slept, your body stayed with freshwater entering the system. Once you take water into your system, it gets your muscles going and provides your body with new energy for the day. One of the biggest indicators of low energy is a dehydrated body. Start your morning refreshed by taking a full glass of pure cold water and observe the wonders it will do for your body.

7. Reduce your screen time

Except if you make your money online or you are an online personality that needs to keep fans updated in real time, then you should keep your phone out of reach in the mornings. Smartphones and social media have been revealed to be some of the biggest killers of productivity and facilitators of procrastination. You can decide to leave your phone in its drawer until lunchtime or put it into airplane mode.

8. Meditate

Meditation will help you tackle stress and anxiety emanating from the previous day. It is best done in the early morning when the world around you is quiet, and your mind is peaceful. Meditation helps you focus your concentration and complete one task at a time, instead of getting pulled over to different tasks. It enables you to stay present in the moment.

9. Streamline your decisions

The morning time comes with a lot of choices: what to wear, where to go, who to call, what to cook, etc. Work on these decisions so that they don't too much of your time each morning and cause you 'decision fatigue.' Have a routine for your morning, such as what to wear and what to eat. Make it simple so that the decision is made quickly and you can go on with your life.

10. Be grateful

Wake up each morning and acknowledge the good things in your life, no matter how small they may be. Take some minutes and practice gratitude. The process is rewarding, and it will provide you with a clearer vision for the day. It will also help you conquer negativity which is one of the hindrances to creativity and productivity.

11. Read a page or two

While exercise sets your body in motion, reading sets your mind into action. People who read are likely to stay ahead of those who do not read. Reading keeps you updated on the latest opportunities available to you and how you can maximize them.

12. Spend time with family

No matter how small it is, this is necessary. Talk to your kids. Laugh with your spouse and get them prepared for the day. A person who leaves home happy is more likely to participate better at work. The genuine happiness from know that joy exists in your family is enough to energize you for the day.

CHAPTER THREE: IGNITING YOUR WILLPOWER

WHAT TO KNOW ABOUT WILLPOWER?

Willpower is the ability to be able to control yourself; but it also goes just beyond ability as it sounds. It is a combination of will and power. Having to do something regular, relaxed, and pleasurable may not task your willpower. Often, your willpower is relaxed in the face of accessible decisions and tasks. The firm determination to do things that are difficult (such as wanting to lose weight or quit drinking alcohol) is the true definition of willpower.

Research has it that a part of your brain (the pre-frontal cortex) powers your willpower just like love and fear is being controlled by the limbic system of the temporal lobe. Willpower feeds on mental energy just like the emotions do, and this can cause you to be tired or fatigued.

I'm sure you can relate to what happens after jogging in the morning for a long time or after doing some push-ups to stay fit. Your muscles become naturally weak then. The same also applies to willpower when the part of the brain that controls it is stressed.

10 POWERFUL STRATEGIES TO INCREASE WILLPOWER

I am about to reveal to you winning rules and tactics to help you hush up the voices that rise against your willpower.

1.   Who are you?

'Man, know thyself' is a famous utterance by the philosopher Socrates. It is of the truth that you alone can tell your high and low points. There are limits to which your abilities can be stretched. You know at what points a joke becomes offensive to you.

Wanting to know yourself could bring you to ask some questions like;

- How far can I go?
- How well can I do?
- Where am I most productive?
- When and where does laziness flourish in me?

2. Self-exploration

Many a time, you face a lot of restraining factors. Most likely, you hear yourself more often than you can count make statements like "I can't go beyond here; I wasn't made for this; I can't do this anymore." The moment the "NOT" word takes center stage in most of your activities, then, you should know that your willpower is on the decline.

Go explore your abilities, push yourself to do unfamiliar feats, and challenge the status quo. In simple terms, push the limits.

3. Stand your ground

"Tomorrow, I will increase my number of sit-ups by ten." "I will start drinking just one bottle of Coke per day from next week." "I will go an extra 200 meters at the next road walk." These are probably things you said but never did. Procrastination is a huge red flag in the path of increasing willpower. The moment you stop saying and start doing is the moment you will begin to record remarkable changes. If you don't stand your ground, the statements will become a popular future recurring rhyme. So, whatever you want to do, start Now!

4. Involve your imagination

Many inventions you find today are as a result of imagination. Someone imagined having to fly in the air as a faster and more convenient mean of transportation rather than drive on the road, and it came to reality. Today, we have the most sophisticated airplanes. Same happens with willpower. The body responds to imaginations just the same way it does to experiences. If you imagined that you fail a test, you would discover that you will begin to feel uneasy, especially if you are the kind of person who detests failing. If you are having a stressed day and you imagine yourself by a pool lying in a recliner with a bottle of chill drink and the feeling of cool breeze, your body will begin to assume that position and feel relaxed. Your body feeds on your imagination. Use the power of imagination to increase your willpower.

5.   Learn to say NO

Most of the challenges faced by your willpower arise from your inabilities to say no to numerous pleasures that come your way. You tend to indulge yourself in too many activities that result into nothing.

6.   Have a recovery strategy

If you want to succeed in increasing your willpower, especially on a long-term basis, then you will need to consider this. Fatigue can also apply to willpower. You may find it rather hard to sustain your willpower if you go on and on so hard without any break or space to recover. It's just a matter of time before you get tired and ultimately fall back to the start. Take some short recovery breaks.

7.   Be conscious of your environment

Pressure and circumstance are vital to increasing your willpower. If you want to achieve or carry out a particular task, make sure you surround yourself with related things or people. If you want to maintain stable mental health, you may as well want to hang around people who are non-toxic and not volatile with whom you can have meaningful and positive conversations. Purge your environment of people and things that tend to want to soften your willpower.

8.   Do it in bits

Willpower can drown in the presence of huge tasks. It is natural to get discouraged at the sight of heavy responsibility. It could even overwhelm you. Why not break it into bits? It is more comfortable and less challenging. Deciding to read a 1000-page book a day can prove to be daunting. However, dividing the book into parts and deciding to read some pages over a specific period feels easier to accomplish.

9.   Set realistic timelines

Even though you are set to increase your willpower, going overboard is not encouraged. Setting unrealistic goals is like "building your castles in the sky."

How do you keep it simple?

- Add a little more time to your reading hours
- Do five more push-ups
- Read one extra book in 2 weeks
- Doing a few more will help you record little but vital progress.

10.   Understand that it is all up to you

Your decision to power up your willpower is yours. You are not in a race with anyone but yourself. Make up your mind to do this for you.

12 GENIUS TRICKS TO FEEL INSTANTLY MOTIVATED

Motivation comes in different forms. It could come like a spark of flame (within seconds or minutes) or gradually like a highly viscous liquid (in hours or days). The good news is that you can ignite any of the two mentioned. For this particular part, here are tips on how to get motivated almost instantly.

1. Eat dopamine-releasing diet

Dopamine is a chemical released by nerve cells and is usually associated with the brain's pleasure and reward system. The release of dopamine in your body creates a feeling of pleasure which motivates you to repeat a pattern of behavior. It means that eating foods that induce the release of dopamine can increase your motivation.

Nonetheless, bear in mind that some diets are capable of reducing the release of dopamine which could cause a reduction in motivation—foods like animal fat, butter, palm oil, and coconut oil fall in this category. It is difficult to avoid these foods altogether, but you can try to reduce their intake significantly. Employ your willpower to achieve this.

2. Take a more motivating posture

In emotional intelligence (EI), mainly when dealing with empathy, nonverbal communication is critical. It is because many important things are left unsaid that being able to figure the unspoken is crucial. The same applies to motivation. Some stances, postures, and body movements can influence your confidence. In other words, it can increase or decrease motivation.

• Sit with your chest pushed out (don't slouch)

Sitting with your chest pushed out (a confident stance) helps you to hold your thoughts with more confidence. Alternatively, if you sit in a slouchy position or with your back curved out, it is perceived as a doubtful posture and would portray a lack of confidence.

Recent studies have shown that sitting slumped in a chair can make one feel less proud of their performance. It can also lead to people giving up quickly on demanding cognitive tasks. So, sit upright.

- **Stand straight with "arms akimbo."**

Standing at "arms akimbo" means standing with the hands placed on each hip in such a way that the elbow flairs out. It translates into taking an expansive posture, which makes the body appear more formidable and taking up more space.

It shows dominance and confidence. The scientific explanation behind this posture is that it boosts testosterone (confidence hormone) and decreases cortisol (stress hormone).

3.   Make positive pronouncements.

"I am making an exponential success," "I can do this because I was made for it," "Nothing can stop my success," "I have what it takes." Saying these things to yourself can greatly motivate you at any time and get you to perform better. Speak to yourself aloud.

4.   Make a deal

When I say the deal, I mean tell a friend about your decision and request him/her to monitor you daily to ensure you are recording improvements. Make it more practical by adding a monetary commitment to the deal.

How do I mean?

Hand over some cash to your friend on conditions that if you can achieve your motivational goal, the money will be returned to you, if not, it should be donated to the charity.

5.   Use the power of positivity to stay motivated

As long as you live, there would always be moments when negativity would set in. Sometimes, your entire day may seem to go wrong. Everything, for whatever reason, would decide to go south. Your boss at work chooses to frustrate every effort you make. Your kids could unexpectedly fall ill. Your colleagues at work appear to irritate you.

The stark truth is that we can't always control circumstances we find ourselves in, but it is our choice how we respond to them. You may find yourself in hard or unpleasant situations. Nonetheless, you will need to decide to stay motivated through them.

Here are some tips on how positivity can help you stay motivated.

- **Surround yourself with positive people**

It is said that "show me your friend, and I will tell you who you are" or you must have heard that "birds of a feather flock together." This implies that your circle of friends or association is an excellent determinant of who you are and how much you can achieve.

On the one hand, if you have around you people who are positive-minded or always optimistic even when it is hard to do so, you will most likely be influenced by their positive vibes. On the other hand, if you have a toxic or pessimistic association, you are bound to stay negative most of the time.

- **Don't dwell on things you can't control.**

There is indeed no perfect condition. Situations that are beyond your control are bound to come up. It is essential to be able to differentiate between things that are within and outside your control, rather than dwell on them or fret over them. If not, you will unnecessarily waste time on them and most likely become stunted.

6.   Have a plan (write it out)

Do you set out for the day's activity without any ideas on how you intend your day to go? How eventually does it turn out? Do you take time to develop a schedule or plan on how you want your week to run?

It is no news that "he who fails to plan, plans to fail."

Making a plan is like having a road map to help you navigate your way into your activity for a period. It gives you a sense of direction. It also helps you cut short the time spent doing nothing or irrelevant things as well as help you enhances your productivity.

Having a plan makes you organized and gives you an inner feeling of satisfaction, especially when you can follow up on your ideas.

- Let's see how you can set up your schedule or plan for a week
- Create a list of activities you wish to carry out for the week
- Narrow the program down to a daily to-do-list
- Allocate a time range to accomplish each task
- Follow upon each task
- Check every assignment as you complete them.

7.   Count your blessings and appreciate your little achievements

Once you can appreciate your little or significant achievements, you will stay motivated to achieve more. It is also important to know that forming the habit of positive reinforcement could be of great help.

Positive reinforcement is rewarding yourself for successes made or achievements recorded. For instance, after a long week of work and having achieved you set goals, you could decide to take yourself out on a treat. Buying yourself something you do not regularly buy or going to places of relaxation and recreation are good examples.

8.   See from a new perspective.

If you have always had negative thoughts or feelings, you could decide to try out a new perspective of being positive. Being positive can alter your life in many ways than you can count. It is also incredibly interesting and exciting to take a positive form.

9.   Try it differently

Having to repeat a routine could be tiring if it is something that would last for an extended period. Why not try it differently? Snap out of the routine. Seeing a situation or task from a different or new perspective could be quite adventurous.

10.   Subscribe to motivational shows and speeches

Listening to motivational talks or reading motivational material can serve as a motivation booster. We are mostly a product of what we hear and read.

11.   Go on an enjoyable and fun activity.

Sometimes, you could feel fatigued or worn out from doing the same thing over and over again. To stay motivated, you can engage in some activities that are fun and relaxing.

You could decide to listen to your favorite songs on your way to work, and you could also decide to take some time out during your break at work to stroll around. The feeling of being out of confinement is refreshing.

During the weekends, you can decide to exercise. Exercises have a way of releasing dopamine, which increases motivation.

12.   Talk to someone

Sometimes, you may fail while trying to motivate yourself even after working so hard to stay positive and motivated. It is ok when you get to this point. Do not beat yourself. Instead, talk to someone you trust. It could be a family member, or you could reach out to a counselor. He/she could guide you on the best approach to return you to motivation.

15 INSPIRATIONAL QUOTES THAT WILL FIRE YOU UP

There are a thousand and one quotes that can shoot you into being motivated to do things you never thought you could. Here are some of the thought-provoking and soul-lifting quote carefully selected.

1.   "If you don't build your dream, someone else will hire you to help them build theirs." —Dhirubhai Ambani

2.   "Don't beg the status quo, challenge it"- Anyanwu Emmanuel

3.   "Whatever the mind of man can conceive and believe, it can achieve." — Napoleon Hill

4.   "Great minds discuss ideas; average minds discuss events; small minds discuss people." — Eleanor Roosevelt

5.   "Have no fear of perfection – you'll never reach it." — Salvador Dalí

6.   "I've failed over and over and over again in my life, and that is why I succeed." — Michael Jordan

7.   "Success is most often achieved by those who don't know that failure is inevitable." — Coco Chanel

8.   "Our greatest glory is not in never falling, but in rising every time, we fall." — Confucius

9.   "Life is 10% what happens to me and 90% of how I react to it." — Charles Swindoll

10.   "The mind is everything. What you think you become." — Buddha

11.   "Start where you are. Use what you have. Do what you can." — Arthur Ashe

12.   "The secret of success is to do the common things uncommonly well." — John D. Rockefeller

13.   "It is hard to fail, but it is worse never to have tried to succeed." — Theodore Roosevelt

14.   "Success is not final; failure is not fatal: it is the courage to continue that counts." — Winston Churchill

15.　　"It had long since come to my attention that people of accomplishment rarely sat back and let things happen to them. They went out and happened to things." — Leonardo da Vinci

CHAPTER FOUR: YOUR DAILY DOSE
OF SELF-DISCIPLINE

Our world today has literarily compelled us to some realities. And the convincing truth about this change is appalling. Think of success as one. To be successful in any job, you must have as an essential ingredient the technical skills to perform effectively. The added spice for excellence is creativity. But not everybody falls into this category. It is not because of anything; it is just that humans have not been able to set goals to achieve this. Setting goals gives you control. There is always a direction to go. It gives you an understanding of where you should start, which turns to take, and finally, your destination is secured. Some even have an idea of setting big targets, but get stuck along the process of achieving those long-term objectives.

There are different ways of achieving goals. Maintaining some goals (which may be a career, life, family, etc.) has on its strategies. This process depends on the person involved since everybody is not on the same level of achievement. Top management level personnel will have concise goals and will be very much useful in achieving it because of many years of setting goals. The experience involved will distinguish the success rate when compared to a lower management level officer.

However, with intense self-discipline, you are sure to maintain these goals effectively. Self-discipline is an essential and useful skill everyone should possess. And as important as this skill is, only a few people acknowledge its importance. Being self-disciplined does not necessarily mean you have to be too hard on yourself or express the same feeling to people around you. It does not mean you should limit your lifestyle to a boring one. The totality of self-discipline is having self-control. It is the ability to measure your inner strength and how it can be transformed to control your actions. You then have a consciousness to react without bias.

Having self-discipline enables you to carry on in decision-making, which helps you accomplish goals with ease. It is more of the inner strength to keep you going. It has control over other inner-core terrible habits. Addiction and procrastination is a deeply rooted habit which self-mastery will help eliminate. That said, it is evident that having self-discipline is necessary for our everyday life.

10 EXPERT TIPS FOR DEVELOPING STRONG SELF-DISCIPLINE

The superb thing about self-discipline is that it is a behavior that can be learned. Our decisions are void of impulses and unsteady feelings. Here are useful tips for developing strong self-discipline.

1. Put A Date On It

Research has shown that putting dates on your activities helps you stay focused and determined to achieve them. It also helps in maintaining a regimen, which, in the long run, helps build strong self-discipline. For instance, you may attach an activity to Mondays, and consistently follow up with it. With enough time, you would have created a regimen for that activity and, in turn, have groomed self-discipline to always perform that activity on Mondays. You might think of fixing Thursdays for your karate class. Once you are committed for the first few weeks, a subconscious knowing will erupt. Even without setting reminders, you get to know that Thursdays is not for a pool party. Get a sticker and fix it on your calendar with the name of the activity. Or you can create a reminder on your mobile devices

2. Identify What Motivates You

Priority is essential in identifying how far you would be self-disciplined. Focus on the most important thing. There is no need to dabble into what will demean and destabilize you. And commitment would not set in if you are unsure of what exactly you need to do. There is always a high possibility of success when there is a feeling of urgency. Clothe yourself with "I must" mentality. "I must always look neat, regardless of how tired I get."

You need motivation to get started. Once you have prioritized your goals, attach modules that keep you going. Your goal might be to get a stable income to maintain a comfortable daily lifestyle. This goal is appropriate and specific. Once you identify that a steady income is essential, it will help you focus on your goals. With this realized, you can control yourself against other things that might have a negative effect on your income. Understand also that you can't be self-disciplined if you are not motivated to continue.

3. Affirm your goals and visualize the benefits you would gain

There should be a plan to achieve your set targets. Most times, we get distracted by the result that we neglect the strategies to make them work.

Analyze how you think this will work well for you. Make sure you are specific as much as possible. Outlined benefits will give you a sense of accountability. Imagine you have highlighted that one of the benefits of eating healthy is good body shape. The moment you start feeding well, and you notice the change in your body, you could quickly tick the benefits as the one you have achieved already. It will push you to a place where you will embrace other interests you have discovered.

Consistently affirm your goals and the benefits you would gain from them. Your mind will repeatedly get in tune with those set targets. If you say every morning, "I am a great athlete because I'll break the record to get a $4,000 scholarship," "I am getting that contract, and it makes me a better engineer." With time, your mind becomes disciplined and determined to achieve these goals.

4. Make Achievable Plans And Stick To Them

Temptations are bound to arise whenever you are determined to achieve a goal. It might be a distraction from social networks or even your friends. Some might also come when it seems you are not making progress. You will understand that this could hinder you from actualizing your targets. However, your goals must be attainable. Don't be ambiguous. Let it be profound to your taste, work condition, lifestyle, and routine. Include precise quantity, time, people, and dates. These variables make it easy to stick to your laid-down formula.

5. Make Your Regimen A Combination Of Things You Need To Do And Things You Want To Do

Management science research has shown that combining these two activities helps form good habits and also helps you quickly achieve the needed. You can get things done, even in the fun of doing other things. Just decide on what can be combined to give you the desired result. For instance, you want to have a girl's day out to talk and have fun. You can choose the same day you have set out for the gym. After some teasing, agree with your friends to go for a workout session. You can even make it competitive. That way, you have achieved an activity you need by combining it with an event you want.

6. Sleep And Eat Well

Lack of proper sleep and food causes the prefrontal cortex (which is responsible for self-regulation) to perform less than expected. Additionally, the ability for a person to focus when they are hungry reduces to the minimum as lack of food causes lack of sugar, which in turn weakens a person. Hunger brings in a sensation of unwillingness. It is always accompanied by tiredness. Your willpower to do anything is being affected. Thus, you are not motivated to concentrate on what you need to do. To stay focused and disciplined, make sure you eat and sleep properly.

7. Reward Every Progress

Do you remember when you were a child and your parents said they would reward you with a gift if you passed your exams? And whenever you pass, and they fulfill their promise, it is always a source of motivation for you to study more? This logic also works for building self-discipline. If you reward yourself for every progress you make, that way you stay motivated to do more, keeping your eyes on the benefits to be gained.

8. Get A Self-Disciplined Circle

External motivation is the first propeller of habit formation. Just as peer pressure can cause a person to form bad habits, having a circle of self-disciplined friends could motivate you to be self-disciplined. Just as the saying goes, "show me your friend, and I would tell you who you are." Put yourself around people who give you a sense of fulfillment. These are people who have the same belief system as you. Even when it seems you are losing willpower, you get to find strength in their resilience. You would get easily encouraged if you found out that your friends have been able to ensure mastery over a particular course you are struggling with.

9. Do It For Yourself

Self-discipline is good, but most importantly, it is best if the purpose is not biased. If you are aiming at getting more disciplined, be sure it is solely a decision made for you. That way, you would appreciate every progress you make. It doesn't mean that you can't seek professional advice or instructions from friends. It just means that you have to be truthful about your action plans without any form of prejudice.

10. Project Future Challenges

You wouldn't want to fall into self-deceit by believing that everything will work as planned. You might stumble, find out what triggered it, and resist falling into the same pit in the future. Forecast other challenges that might arise as you go on the journey of self-discipline. Think of distractions and problems. They don't have to subdue you. Create a plan to tackle it.

7 DAILY PRACTICES TO KEEP BUILDING SELF-DISCIPLINE

Self-discipline cannot be attained in a day. It requires consistency and perseverance, and daily practices can only build this. Commit yourself to know that the journey to maximum self-discipline is not a palatable one, but the end is always a meal to remember. Here are the daily practices you can use in building your self-discipline.

1. The Cold Bath Test

Everyone hates a cold bath, especially in the morning. That icy blast hitting your face when you are still trying to keep your eyes open can be pretty annoying. It requires a lot of resolution and discipline to subject yourself to that icy blast every morning. And if you can pull through it each morning, that is another step to maximum self-discipline. Prepare your mind for the fact that self-discipline wouldn't look appealing at the start. And it may even become burdensome and time-consuming as time progresses. It will require you a lot of patience and commitment, especially if it is not within your culture. But in the end, you will have more reasons to stay disciplined.

2. **Daily Meditation**

Sitting at a spot with your eyes closed and just listening to your breathing might appear dumb at first. But do you know that meditation is a great way to build self-mastery? Because it requires a high level of concentration for you to sit at a spot and consciously listen to your breath? Consider doing this practice every day, and you will increase the strength of self-discipline. Additionally, meditation helps clear your mind, which in turn enables you to reconnect with your inner self. Try sitting and listening to your breath every morning. After some weeks, you would have disciplined your mind to focus on your inner self and would have built your self-discipline through this exercise.

3. **Identify Your Weaknesses**

Every human being has weaknesses, and most of us tend to overlook them. Being disciplined means you understand your flaws, challenges, and weaknesses, yet are determined to overcome them. If you are a "glutton" but are committed to stop eating out of proportion, the first step is to acknowledge your problem. "Is it that I like to taste everything I see, or I don't get satisfied when I eat more of carbohydrates" Then, ask yourself, "how can I solve this problem?" Having acquired a solution, consciously follow up on it by having in mind the picture of the result (less weight). Admitting these flaws is the first step to overcoming them. Hence, to attain the maximum state of self-discipline, you must acknowledge that there is a need for it and the hindrances stopping you from achieving it.

4. Run Every Morning

A one-mile sprint takes about six to ten minutes and a new determination to pull through. It might appear hard to accomplish at first, but it is a useful tool for building endurance and discipline. Sprinting every morning gives you an automatic jump start for the day and enough energy to pull through it. Be sure you do it before the cold bath in other to maximize your self-discipline growth. If you are reluctant to do this alone, speak to a friend about it and both of you can get started. Ensure that your aim of running is fulfilled.

5. Make Your Bed

Everyone wants to wake up and jump off their beds and get on with their day. No one sees the need to take about two to three minutes to make their beds. Hence, it requires a lot of discipline to consciously decide to make your bed. Always convince yourself that it is necessary to fix your bed because it promotes a positive habit of neatness. The good thing is that it takes very little time. A conscious effort to do it every morning can improve your self-discipline significantly.

6. Eliminate Temptations

Temptations and distractions kill discipline. Without them, attaining maximum self-discipline is possible. However, their presence causes you to either be sluggish or give up. Every distraction or temptation is unique to each goal, and understanding them helps you eliminate them and stay on course, thereby building your self-confidence. Whenever you are tempted or discouraged, remind yourself that, "this is the best time to give my best."

Affirmations by itself will not eradicate temptations. Analyze those things that get you obsessed. Clear them and refuse to go alongside that direction. If you are trying to read, stay away from the PlayStation. Video games will not help you focus during exams.

Make a schedule of when to hang out with friends if you see yourself wasting a productive moment with a close acquaintance. If you are having trouble studying an e-book on your phone because of updates of an adventure game, force close the app or uninstall it if necessary.

Let temptation be a positive reminder that you have been doing well, and this time is not the moment to give up.

7. **Be Intentional About Your Goals**

Getting an all-around commitment to daily targets is necessary for achieving more excellent results. You wouldn't be the best version of yourself when you have not been purposeful about your goals. Start by making it clear. Write them down. Your journal or notepad can be an excellent place to pen it down. You can as well write down any affirmations you think will motivate you to keep going.

20 POSITIVE AFFIRMATIONS TO INSPIRE SELF-DISCIPLINE

Whatever you say consistently to yourself sticks in your mind permanently. It creates a consciousness in which you work in. This is why assertions are a significant part of building self-discipline. Every day when you wake up, say these affirmations to yourself.

1. I am a fantastic person, and I am thankful for this opportunity to grow.

2. I am determined to make myself better mentally, spiritually and emotionally.

3. I must work on myself. I am doing the right thing.

4. This day is an excellent day for me, and I am going through it with a spirit of gratitude.

5. I adjust to who I am becoming: my strength motivates me, and my weaknesses are a discouragement to me. I overcome every fault. My shortcomings are turned to advantages.

6. On this day, I am intentionally defining boundaries and eliminating every form of distraction and temptation.

7. I have complete control of my time, and today I am not engaging in any bad habit.

8. I am strong and capable of becoming self-disciplined. And I would attain my maximum state of self-discipline

9. At every point in time, I know what I am expected to do, and that is what I would do.

10. I am accomplishing every task I have today. I am conscious of the benefits of living healthy. Therefore, I am guided to eat right.

11. I am giving my best at everything I do today. I prosper at the work of my hands.

12. Today, as I decide to do my daily routine, I achieve all that is set before me. I am organized and prompt in every area of my life.

13. No challenge can pull me down. I surmount every difficulty. Natural circumstances do not move me.

14. Worry will not solve my problems. Therefore, I will not be anxious about anything.

15. My imagination is active. I use my imaginative power to create excellence. My mind is open to receive new ideas. I am quick to act on positive impulse. I am motivated from within. Nothing can stop me!

16. My mind is attracted to positivity. I do not see negativity. I am making progress with giant strides.

17. I affirm that I am an advantage in my world. This is not the time to give up on myself. I am not ordinary. I am undaunted by challenges

18. I reign in life. All things work together for my good. I am strengthened and energized for victory today.

19. I am life-conscious. My body is energetic and full of vitality. There is no space for sickness, disease, infirmity, or anything that brings pain to my body.

20. Nothing can pull me down. I do not see the present temptation. I am full of benefits.

CHAPTER FIVE: FINDING FOCUS

The average human has a short attention span that doesn't even last a mere eight minutes. Surprisingly, that is the attention span of a goldfish. Because of your digital life, this number has shrunk even further. The brain is always on the lookout for the next exciting thing happening in the environment. We are most likely to get bored because of this.

Your ability to focus and pay attention to your environment is essential to your survival. It is a skill, and you have to improve it to make it better. Focus is just like the muscular system of the body. The more it is exercised, the stronger and more substantial it becomes. The process of focus building is a mental battle that you have to partake in to better your self. Don't dwell on the idea that you are the kind of person who easily loses focus. Buying into that narrative will spell doom for you.

The question now remains, how can focus be built and developed? In an age where everything is vying for your attention and pulling you in different directions, what can be done to keep your mind at alert?

10 ATTENTION EXERCISES TO BUILD CONCENTRATION

As I mentioned before, your mind and concentration strength can be exercised to increase the value. Just like a gym instructor will dish out exercises for you to do to develop different parts of your muscular system, there are some other exercises for the mind that can be used to build your "concentration system." Remember, your success mostly depends on how well you can concentrate and capture the details that surround you. Here are some of those exercises you can do.

1. **Exercise One:** Take a book or magazine and open it to any page you may find interesting. Read up that page and

understand its content. Begin to count the words on the page, one paragraph after another. As you count, take note of each word contained in each paragraph. Try to understand their function in each sentence. Then go over and make a recount. Once you notice that you can easily count the words in the first paragraph, you can move over to the next.

2. **Exercise Two:** Count the numbers backward from 100 to 1. Make a picture of each number as you count and do this as fast as you can. Concentrate your mind on picturing the whole numbers in a line of ten. Increase your count to a range of 500 and 1000.

3. **Exercise Three:** Take an object and focus the whole of your mind on it. It could be a fruit, a toy, or any other object. Observe its components and features, the things that make up this particular object. Take note of its shape, color, size, flaws, and all. Continue to pick out all of these things and don't allow your mind to wander while you do this. Even if it does, bring back to base. Do this for three minutes at a time and continue to increase until you finally master it.

4. **Exercise Four:** The next time will be to visualize the object you have just observed. Close your eyes for a while and try to picture what you have studied for some time. How go does your mind bring back the image to you? Try to bring back all of those things that you discovered while observing the object. If your mind fails to produce a clear model, open it up for a while and observe again. Then close your eyes and see how well the image forms. Do this repeatedly until you are finally able to picture the object in its full form.

5. **Exercise Five:** Choose a particular word or phrase in your mind and keep repeating it to yourself in your mind. Do this silently without causing any attention towards yourself. Do this until your mind learns to concentrate throughout the process for about ten minutes.

6. **Exercise Six:** You can play a small game with your nose. When going through a flower garden or the local park, keep your nose open and ready to grasp the different types of flower smell that can be detected. This exercise requires some level of concentration to differentiate the various scents in the environment.

7. **Exercise Seven:** Take a good position and stay quiet. You can either lie down flat or sit on a chair. Do not move as you remain in that position. Keep your full concentration on your heartbeat. Try to picture the mechanism of blood flow throughout your system and try to figure out where the blood reaches around your body. With constant practice, you will soon be able to feel your blood flowing through your body.

8. **Exercise Eight:** Practice the art of self-control. You might be the kind of person with a strong desire to talk and spill secrets about others. By learning to control these urges, you will be able to energize your concentration strength. To continually put these things behind your mind and force them to remind there is so much power than you can understand. It will help you put your will and desire in check. No matter how exciting the news may be, try your possible best to keep it under wraps until the appointed time for which it should be revealed.

9. **Exercise Nine:** Try to keep your mind void of any form of thought. This is probably going to be the hardest of all the other activities. Your mind is constantly being bombarded with ideas, and to keep them out requires a lot of concentration. Try to do this for one minute at a time. Once you conquer that timeframe, you can go on to five minutes and then ten minutes.

10. **Exercise Ten:** Engage in art. Art here does not only refer to painting, drawings, or sculptures. Art is a whole lot wider than that. Art is in your everyday conversation. Art is in the movies you watch and the song you listen to. Pay closer

attention, and don't just do these things because you are bored. You might not know what you can discover, and you will ultimately learn concentration by paying attention to these little things.

5 MINDFULNESS EXERCISES TO BUILD FOCUS

Focus is considered an essential ingredient to success in life or any endeavor. Focus is a rudiment to the improvements of your thinking mechanisms such as your learning ability, perception strength, and problem-solving. Learning to build focus becomes very important when these factors are considered. Focus helps you achieve mental clarity. There are several ways with which you can start practicing how to create focus and use it to complete any given task.

Mindfulness in this regard refers to a state of being present in the moment. It is being aware and open at the moment. Mindfulness deters your mind from wandering around and losing its place.

1. **Exercise One:** You are never your best whenever you are in a hurry. When you slow down, you learn to reconnect with the environment. Slow down as you walk through the driveway. Don't chew your food too fast. Take your mind and appreciate the world around you. Slowing down does not mean that you are sluggish or a sloth, slowing down is looking deeper and preventing mistakes. Remember what they say: Slow and steady wins the race.

2. **Exercise Two:** What do you see when you close your eyes. What lies behind your closed eyelids? The eyes are a major source of distraction to the mind. Close your eyes and cut away that distraction. Close your eyes and focus on the pictures in your mind. Listen to the sounds around you. Your other senses perform better once your eyes are close, so close them and see what you can discover.

3. **Exercise Three:** Train your eyes to catch the footprints pattern. Learning footsteps is one right way to understand

human and animal nature. Footsteps are like messages that need to be deciphered. If you can train your mind and eyes to catch things as small and seemingly insignificant as footstep pattern, it will be quite easier to pick the essentials.

4. **Exercise Four:** Every time we are prone to emotions which we may not necessarily understand. We might soon find ourselves not paying attention to what we feel. This exercise involves you finding a name for your emotion and pinpointing the reason why you feel that way.

5. **Exercise Five:** Observe the people around you. You can practice in an office or in any public space. Keep your eyes on one person and note what they are doing. Observe their body language and their dress pattern. Try to keep a picture of them in your mind, so that forget them once you take your eyes away. Become more mindful of the people around you and the actions they carry out.

10 WAYS TO CONQUER DISTRACTIONS

Most of the time, we start with good intentions of having our minds on the task at hand, but something happens are we soon discover that we have lost focus. You know that you have the ability, the strength, and the drive to carry on, but distractions always have the upper hand and soon you notice that you have been overpowered. Think of distractions as small pests in your workplace that bore holes and prevent productivity. If you do nothing about them, they grow stronger and continue to build their net over you. If only you can take some time off and try to calculate how many hours you have lost to distractions, you will understand how bad the situation has become. And the truth is that distractions are so powerful, and conscious efforts needs to be made to be able to conquer them. Some of these strategies will help you stay on top and overcome distractions:

1. **Identify your sources of distraction:** Different people have different things that distract them. For some, it would be watching ballet dance videos on YouTube, while for others, it would be their own thoughts. All you need to do first is to identify what constitutes a distraction to you. This is the first step to take to eliminate these pests.

2. **Develop distraction-proof habits:** There are small habits built over time that can help you become a better person overall. For these habits to grow, first you must create a friendly environment devoid of distraction for them. It is never an easy task, and it will require a lot of work. Small things like ads block and switching off your phone can help you build these habits. Other people around you should have an idea that you have entered a distraction-free mode and you can get them informed with simple acts like closing your office door or putting on a headphone. Put away anything that can serve as a source of distraction, and your mind will begin to learn that it can do without those distractions.

3. **Keep your mind in check:** Your thoughts are some of the most subtle sources of distractions. Watch how your mind begins to wander when you are carrying out the most serious activities, even during an exam. We spend a good percentage of our mind thinking about something else while carrying out a task. The key here is to notice when the mind is about to begin the journey and hold it back. This will mean paying a lot of attention to your mind. If there is a problem at hand that your mind keeps going back to, then you should find a solution to that problem and free your mind.

4. **Don't multitask:** Myths are flying around about the benefits of multitasking. Although some people are very proficient in the act, I do not endorse it. Multitasking is not only a distraction but a clear source of fatigue to the brain. You might feel like you have achieved more when you multitask, but when you go back, you will discover a lot of mistakes

with than things that you may have thought you did right. Stopping one task and starting up another is a brain drain and focus can easily be lost.

5. **A short break will do you good:** Whenever you notice yourself getting distracted, you can take a short break and reassess the work at hand. Try to recapture the reasons why you have to remain focused on your job and give your mind a reason to concentrate. Your brain needs to be reminded about why the task at hand is important and why distractions should not even be an option.

6. **Break down the tasks into smaller fragments:** Distractions are more prone to present themselves when a project seems overwhelming. It is better for tasks to be broken down into smaller projects so that the brain is deceived into thinking the job is easier and will take a much smaller timeframe. With each accomplished project, you fell a sense of accomplishment that drives you to do more.

7. **Set Deadlines for each task:** Don't just start up a task without a deadline. Timing is everything. Give your mind and brain a timeframe to complete the task. This will give a sense of urgency, and your mind will be eager to get the job quicker.

8. **Set yourself apart:** This one goes for people who are prone to get distracted when people are around them. It is necessary to have people around you at all times, but you should also be able to identify when they constitute a distraction in your life. Before you start up a task, you can tell the people around you about how important at hand is and how much space you would love to be given. Or you can take yourself away from them until you get the job done. They might not understand how important it may before you to complete that task successfully.

9. **Track the daily pattern of your life:** It would make sense for you to track each day's activities at night to find out how

much time was spent doing what. This evaluation will quickly help you identify the distraction patterns in your life that you need to combat. When these habits have been identified, you can now start working towards creating habits that will eliminate their effect.

10. **Start early:** Earlier in this book, we talked about staying in bed until your body is ready to get up. But sometimes you need to push your body out of bed to get things done. This period of the day is best used to get your day started. There are hardly any distractions at this point, and your mind is most active and ready to perform.

7 FOODS THAT CAN HELP BOOST YOUR BRAINPOWER

You should do everything to protect your brain and help boost its operating power. The importance of your brain cannot be overemphasized. It is in charge of a whole lot of things that go on around your body. When all of these are considered, you now discover why it is quite important to keep your brain in peak working function.

Some foods can be taken to get the brain working at its best. These foods have a lot of impact on the structure and the health of the brain. They also have some minor and major nutrients that are needed by the brain to perform to optimum levels. It has been proven over time that our body parts begin to deteriorate as we grow old, and this includes the brain, too. But even with this, you can help your brain to maintain its health as you learn to eat smarter. Some of these foods can help your brain perform better:

1. **Blueberries**

Research has shown that the flavonoids produced by this fruit are very for memory improvement. They are also known to protect the brain and reduce the effects of Alzheimer's disease and dementia. The brain also needs the antioxidants produced by the blueberries and to help improve communication among the brain cells. You can add them to your early morning cereal or squeeze out their juice.

2. Fatty Fish

The omega-3 fatty acids contained in fatty fish are known to reduce the quantity of beta-amyloid in the bloodstream. This beta-amyloid is a form of protein that forms lumps in blood vessels and the brain, thereby causing Alzheimer's disease. Omega-3 fatty acid also helps to increase the blood flow towards the brain. Some of these fishes include sardines, tuna, sardines, and salmon.

3. Broccoli

Glucosinolates contained in broccoli is broken down by the body to form isothiocyanates. These isothiocyanates are known to reduce the possibility of degenerative diseases occurring in the body. Broccoli is also very rich in flavonoids and vitamin C, which are also necessary for the brain health.

4. Turmeric

Curcumin contained in turmeric enters the brain to directly benefit the cells reproducing there. Curcumin is a potent antioxidant and anti-inflammatory compound that benefits memory system in the brain. Studies have also shown that it helps to improve the mood when it is taken.

5. Whole Grains

Whole grains are known to contain a lot of vitamins which is very important for the development of the brain and the neurological system. Whole grains include foods like barley, rice, oatmeal, and whole-grain pasta. Some of them can be taken as early cereal, or they can be boiled and taken with sauce. It is all left to your culinary imaginations.

6. Kale

Kale is another vegetable that contains glucosinolates, and just like broccoli they are also known to help reduce the body's susceptibility to degenerative diseases and keep the brain healthy and ready to function.

7. Green Tea

Caffeine, which is very important for brain function, can be found in Green tea. Taking green tea in the morning can help to give the brain a dose of alertness, memory, and focus. Another essential nutrient in green tea is L-theanine. L-theanine is an amino acid that promotes the activities of the neurotransmitter GABA. L-theanine can also help the brain relax when there has been an insanely stressful activity.

CHAPTER SIX: DEFEATING BAD HABITS

By now, you must have been practicing the tips given in chapters four and five about self-discipline and staying focus. Nevertheless, a conscious effort must be taken to sustain what has been learned. Thorough and sustained learning requires the learner to understand the position at which he is learning. Knowing your pace and the attitude involved is a good starting point. As it is not enough to acquire new set skills but also to identify those negative behavior pattern that ruins your productivity. These are setbacks that have been a part of your life. But what happens when you discover that the negative attitudes that frustrate your learning process are your habits? And these habits, as at when realized, have reduced the pace at which your productivity level is achieved. Our attention is not on when the bad habits started, as some began theirs at a tender age while others developed theirs as they grew into adulthood. It is a good thing that it is discovered and your statistics must have summarized the effect per time, ranging from emotional, psychological, health, etc.

Bad habits have a way of dealing with us. Some start with our inner self. It proceeds to destroy our self-image and self-worth while many others reflect on our productivity level. Whatever the effect might be, you can defeat it. You would want to know that the adverse impact of these bad habits can be so dangerous that they affect your health and mental state. And an unhealthy being can't perform to the best of his abilities.

12 BAD HABITS THAT ARE KILLING YOUR PRODUCTIVITY

1. Trying to do every task

Humans are not robots. And no one anticipates you to do everything. Even robots are programmed for a specific job. But more frequently than not, you tend to overwork yourself by trying out every task.

Trying something new is not bad, but doing every task is the problem. You tend to lose focus when you do that. You won't be able to boast of specialization. It would be wrong if a sales manager is seen performing the task of a personnel admin. Just as you can't eat everyone's food, so can't you do every job.

2.   Letting social networks distract you

Everyone is excited at the new interface that comes with the latest update, the added filters that beautifies the sight and the one-time swipe function. And since work has taken the space of your intimate friends, getting another acquaintance who wouldn't leave anytime soon is inevitable. You then spend more of your time with them to the extent that it becomes a habit. That feeling of excitement that comes from sticking to your digital friends on the different social media platforms and the trends and updates has always been a major killer to your productive moment.

3.   Clutter

You might not think of confusion as a big deal until you figure out that you can't get what you want without looking for it. Why? Because it is not organized as it ought to. An office cabinet filled with outdated reports, newspapers, and journals can add up to your work. It presents to your partner how disorganized you are. All office documents have their filing system. Littering it up with other irrelevant kinds of stuff makes everywhere untidy, and you will always need to hand yourself a search warrant.

4.   Lack of a plan

Waking up into the day with the right mental attitude is good. But having no intention to fulfill the day is not a good thing to bank on. Sticking to the general plan or a plan of "no plan" is a bad habit you need to eliminate. You can't go with the flow when there is a goal to achieve. What if the general plan is not fit for your specific task?

5. Thinking of work every time

The main passion that fuels your job is the love that you have for it. But this love cannot be productive if it is not well-expressed. Thinking of work every time leaves you worried. You tend to ask yourself multiple questions at a time. What do I do next? What about the report? How do I present this paperwork? And so on. It then distracts you from creating time to plan for the work. What you have been doing is mainly anxiety.

6. First thing last, the last thing first

This sequence is a total reversal of priority. Everyone wants something, but not everyone has been able to pin their specific needs down according to how bad they need them. Generalizing what you need may not help you to do things differently. Imagine giving too many options when you can structure your needs down to the order of its importance.

7. Easy task first, hard ones later

The hard task is technically challenging, and that's why it's called that name. People tend to push the more difficult task to the future whereas, those are the most important. Getting to do the more straightforward job first, without creating a strategic plan on how to solve the harder one, pushes the task to a tight corner. It becomes harder every time it gets pushed back. Pushing an essential task to the future wouldn't make you achieve your aim. It even adds more pressure to the job.

8. Complaints

Our mental and psychological state in the workplace could be affected most times, and it is just natural for humans to get tired. And one attitude that reflects tiredness is the vocal utterance that accompanies it. Mumbling and soliloquy is a common symptom. Complaints come from a negative feeling when the right results are not achieved. And the effects of these feelings result in an unwillingness to finish the task.

9.   The perfect little bit

Dedication is an attribute that shows that you value your work. This catalyst might sometimes involve adding spices to the bit that makes up perfection. Perfection is what defines our excellence. But it would be burdensome when we tend to spice up all the bits. And the bits in itself is unimportant to the result intended. What happens is that we get stuck? We get frustrated, right? Then, stress pops in.

10.   Negativity

Negativity is more of a mind thing than a physical thing, the result of which is visibly assessed. It all starts with the wrong mentality to progressively have a poor outcome. Most times, it doesn't come because someone inspired it. It comes as a reminder in your mind. It allows you to blame yourself, put yourself down. You then conclude that you are not fit to meet the target or to do any extraordinary thing. What happens is that the result will be reduced.

11.   Between the fence

A lot of times, we are faced with a great decision to make. These are choices that determine the progress of our success or an entirely purposed success. It might even be a concern that stems from the outside world but affects our immediate. A good example is when you are faced with a decision to execute a project with a handful of clients. Those which have different variables such as technicality, speed, experience, expertise, and so on. But no one wants to make the mistake of choosing the wrong one. However, not making one at all wouldn't complete the task. Your indecisiveness even prolongs the completion date.

12.   Little time to rest

A power nap is believed to revive energy and set you up to start an excellent task. So, what happens if all you got left after a hectic day is just a little time to rest? Most times, the office job is taken home as overtime. But we tend not to get the best out of the task because our body system has not been revitalized. This routine is a nasty habit that needs a second thought.

6 WAYS TO ELIMINATE BAD HABITS NOW

Eliminating bad habits is a great decision to take. Some have, over time, chosen to ignore their bad habits because they consider it a proper way of life. Others have found measures to manage it. Either way, life can be lived to the fullest when you are confident that no negative attitude is eating you up. Understand that it is quite possible to eliminate bad habits, and you need to be ready to do this. The following can be employed as a guide to help you out.

1.   Getting ready

A great way to start a task is when you are fully aware of the task at hand. The same thing is with eliminating bad habits. Prepare yourself for this task. Preparing yourself means saying, "I am ready for this, and there is no better time than now." Come to the full understanding that you have signed up to do the better thing. Let it start from within you. Just like when you are inclined to think otherwise, align yourself with this new mentality that "This is my perfect time to eliminate those bad habits, and I am getting better." You might be tempted to weigh your options. Don't give it a shot. Put everything in place to get you going.

•   Think differently

Human beings are naturally comfortable when things are easy. And for you, the bad habits must have given a bit of comfort. It's high time to think differently about the whole situation. Have a mindset that you are fighting a battle with your bad habits. Think of yourself as the soldier that is equipped with the modern-day armory and your bad habits have only stone-age weapons. With this mindset alone, you have already placed yourself in a position of victory. All other steps that will be taken will not be considered grievous.

- **Intentionality**

A deliberate attitude needs to be asserted here. You need to stand for this new movement regardless of any challenge that may accompany this exercise. Activate the power of the mind to achieve the great result of breaking those bad habits

2. The Snail Approach

If there is anything the snail is known for, it is its slowness in movement. No one is suggesting to you to get a snail (you might if you want to). But the snail approach brings an understanding that you have to start small. And starting small sometimes might appear slow. Understand that your new habit will not come as a "big bang" but in a steady-state. Your aim at this level is progress. Ensure that you are doing something different from the old habit. There is no need to rush.

3. Identify the why

You might not have thought about why you do the things you do, maybe just because it has become a part of you. Get settled and identify those things that trigger you to do what you do. Maybe you overthink your job anytime you receive a new mail. Or you actively stay on social networks whenever you have a dispute with your friend. Just identify the triggers behind those bad habits, and you have started the elimination process already.

- **Evaluate**

A sincere appraisal of your negative behavior is necessary at this stage. Sincerely weigh the consequences of these behaviors with the right one. You would agree that the positive sides far outweigh the negative. Don't crucify yourself when you have a setback. It is an expectation that is likely to happen. Ensure you get back on track

4.   Create reminders

One of the first drives that support our commitment is when we are constantly reminded of it. You need to be reminded that you want to eliminate these bad habits. It will not only help you at present, but will also create an atmosphere for a great future.

•   Digital reminders

Pushing a reminder can work well with most mobile devices. You can search for apps that create a to-do list, look up the options and enable the alarm function. Create a word or phrase that continually reminds you of the habit to break. It's quite evident that, by now, you must have identified the cause or triggers of your bad habit. If yours is staying on the social networks often, you may want to have a word that says, "it's time to sleep." Or if you are fond of negativity, you might have this: "My negative thought pattern will not help me, I deserve happiness, and that's what will work for me." Ensure you set the alarm at least 10 minutes before the beginning of your extremes. You will know when you are about getting there. This well-structured strategy will create enough time for you to adjust effectively.

•   Journaling

Writing things out yourself will give you a sense of personalizing your target. Get a journaling book in the book store or create one for yourself. Divide the page into two vertically. Start with writing your noted terrible habits on the first side. Add reminders of what you should do (or not do) on the other side. This idea models the digital reminder. You could analyze your progress by ticking the habit you are constantly reminded of.

- **Friends**

You might consider telling your friend about this move. There is always a friend that pushes us until a task is done successfully. He/she might even come up with better suggestions or plan. This action will give you a sense of accountability. Ensure you inform your friend to provide you with a progress report, or you could come up with a guide yourself. He wouldn't want you to be ridiculed with failure. Not again!

- **Stickers**

Inscribe short words/phrases on labels and fix it around you. The little sticky note scattered around you will serve a perfect reminder of what you need to do. Ensure you attach it where your bad habit triggers. It can be in your office, on your calendar, notepad, on the wall and even in your car.

5.   Switch your surroundings

Visiting a particular place might be the trigger to one of your bad habits. You tend to drink more bottles of beer whenever you hang out with friends at the local bar downtown. Consider going to another bar, different from the one you frequent, this time alone. Create a new atmosphere for yourself. Sometimes, the feel of a place you continuously visit pushes you to react negatively.

- **Rewarding every broken habit**

"Broken habit" here means that you have been able to stop the practice successfully. You are no longer seen doing it. Motivate your progress into positivity by rewarding yourself. Everyone needs encouragement. And this reward system may be the only thing that will keep you going till you achieve maximum success.

- **Substitute**

A meaningful way to reward yourself is to look for a positive habit that will substitute the bad habit. A habit is a part of your life. Just like the game of football, the less effective player is replaced; but in urgent cases, a dire need to change the fit player is inevitable when the strategy does not seem to work. It is the same here. Change the less productive habit to have a more productive life.

You would also agree that those bad habits come with fulfillment. Most times, it is there to fulfill a need that might come as a result of depression, sadness, rejection, failure, boredom, etc. if those needs are not met with another thing, then, there is a loophole.

- **Draft a plan and strategize**

Know what to do the when triggers immediately come up. Work with the strategy of reward system any time you replace your bad habit with the positive pattern. Don't give space for loneliness. Loneliness in this regard means dissatisfaction in your expectations. Don't expect to be in that mess again. This practice would be quite more comfortable for you when you avoid the triggers

- **Look out to the future**

The future you are looking out for is someone else's reality, and some people are doing what you want to achieve now. Why not move close to them and make new friends. If restraining yourself from your old friends will give you enough time to break off from your bad habits, you need to give it a shot.

6.   Seek professional support

If you still find it challenging to adopt a positive attitude towards the effort of helping yourself, consider seeing a professional. The psychologist can help identify psychological, emotional, and behavioral patterns that trigger bad habits. He will ensure your progress and can be accounted to.

6 WAYS TO CREATE GREAT HABITS THAT STICK

You may have wondered why your plans are not working as expected. It may have worked for some time, but it looks dull and does not seem to work. You may have told yourself to stop staying 8 hours a day on the internet without learning something new, but it seems not to work. Do not fret. Come to a new awareness that this is a different game for you. It's not the game of chance but total commitment. Be sure that you have been able to discover what triggers your bad habits and the estranging patterns behind it. You might need to analyze your pursuit and the sacrifice behind it. "What do I want and how bad do I want it to change my life?" Have a breakdown of what you will be doing more and what will be done less. Tell your inner self the truth that needs to be told. This is you looking forward to the future of positivity. This is a sure way to get started.

1.　　Focus on one habit at a time

Since your habits didn't start all at once, you need to know that changing it won't be all at once either, as much as you want it to be. Try tackling one habit at a time. If your focus is to stop the negative attitude towards project execution, face it. Don't combine many things. It's even an unhealthy attitude to try doing many things together

Start with the habit you are most uncomfortable with. Don't be in a rush. Progress is what you are after. Once you know the course you are following, getting there won't be a problem.

2.   Ask questions

Don't act as if you are a professional here. There are so many things that will be going through your mind. Ask! You might be wondering how you would survive the night without excessive alcohol. Ask: "What if I would survive the first four hours?" Asking questions should not be limited to you. The help of a therapist or psychologist could be of help. You could also find it helpful when you ask questions from someone who has stuck to the new habit you are about to learn.

Your curiosity might also want to know when you will be able to adapt to the new habit. Ask! This way, you can make up your mind since you know the "when," "how," and "why."

3.   Start with a deadline
We have established that there is no need to rush through sticking to positive habits. But you can start small and at your own pace. Give yourself a deadline to try out the first habit. Let's say for twenty days. So, for the next twenty days, you won't make that specific habit you have decided to start with. And of course, you'd replace it with the positive one. You can monitor your progress with your fingers. Your fingernails can represent the first ten days. Get a designed nail sticker and fix it to your fingernails daily after successfully sticking to the positive habit. After the sticker must have been attached for the first ten days, start removing them daily till the end of the next ten days. This action plan will give you a sense of control. You will have been able to both personalize this exercise and at the same time give it a deadline.

4.   Celebrate your progress
You have started on a "big cheque" "less work" model. The big cheque represents your aspired habit, while less work is your effort to make things better. Realize that your goal is big but achievable. Achieving your aim progressively shows that you have moved from

the realm of fantasy to reality. So why not celebrate every purpose you achieve? Boost your motivation by celebrating every progress. This tells you that you can do more and even better.

5.   Stay with the tune

The rhythm of the new habit has been on the air for some time. Make sure you continue to dance to the song. No other song should persuade you. You have to be consistent. You might not want to change your routine. Try to build your purposed habit according to your method. All you require to do is to put on the new initiative. You might be thinking of decluttering your wardrobe. You could effectively do this the very moment you want to dress up. Just pick your preferred dress and use the other hand to arrange the other suits. Remember, start small so that you won't be overwhelmed.

6.   Don't give too many options

Being specific on strategies to stick to your new habit is necessary. Once you decide on how you want to go about it, stick to the plan. The moment you start weighing many options, doubt may set in. You might even get confused and discouraged. You have decided to reduce your alcohol intake by taking one full lemon after a glass of beer. Good! Stick to it. There are many other important decisions to make than to begin to conflict the ones you have already made.

CHAPTER SEVEN: TAMING THE MIND

The human mind is naturally wild and always in need of an adventure. Because of this, it is necessary that you learn how to tame the mind and have it work to your advantage. This will help it work to your advantage and provide you with lots of positivity. One of the wisest teachers and psychologists of all time, Buddha, described the human mind as a monkey that is always jumping about screeching and chattering endlessly. We all have minds that never want to rest, always in need of something else. Just as a monkey is always in need of attention, the human mind to always want you to put your entire focus on it. It achieves its goals in different ways, such as overhanging, negative considerations, anxiety, and fear.

Due to the presence of this monkey mind, it has now become harder for us to live in the present. Most of our time as humans is spent either regretting about the past or living in fear of the future. Soon you discover that you have become unhappy, sad, naturally angry, and restless. It is time to calm down and tame the monkey in mind. After all, it is your mind, and you should make use of it like you actually possess it. Some simple benefits of taming your mind include:

- Clarity of mind
- Full happiness
- Better sleep
- Focus and concentration
- etc.

All of these are very excellent benefits, and you should not hesitate to embrace them into your life. But there are some minor steps I will show you to help you fully actualize this dream.

12 ESSENTIAL TIPS TO STOP OVERTHINKING AND CONTROL YOUR MIND

It might sound strange to you, but the truth is that you are probably addicted to thinking. You may have never started to consider it, but most of us do spend a lot of time thinking and overworking our minds. We think about what to eat for dinner, which seasons to continue on Netflix, why the world climate is changing so severely. We think about virtually everything. While thinking is an excellent and necessary venture, it can sometimes clog up the mind when it becomes too much. Most of the time, we never know that it has become too much, and that is where the problem lies. Thinking so much in your mind can become a slight disorder and turn you towards overwhelming anxiety. Your mind stays stressed, and peace begins to elude you. Practice these and come up with your testimony:

1. **Study your mind and find those things that cause you stress and anxiety**

There are different reasons for different people as to why they overthink. For some, it could be financial instability; for others, security reasons; and for still others, it could be a terminal sickness. You will need to find yours. Ask yourself the necessary questions why you overthink, and the times you are most likely to overthink. Take note of the major things you think of and the pattern in which all of those thoughts form themselves. If this is done diligently, your notes will help you figure out some of the major reasons why you are currently overthinking.

2. **Consider the things that make you overthink**

The question here is, how important are those things that make you overthink? What use will they play in your life is you continue to trouble your mind about them? Will it matter in four years or four months even? If the answer is no, you should snap out of it. Your mind is simply playing sad tricks with you, and you have to be the boss here. If they are not important, then you should stop thinking about them and focus your time on more important things.

3. Make quick decisions

Learn to make a quick decision and get the process over with. If you are a kind of person that can take hours trying to figure out what to eat for lunch, then this is for you. There should be a timeframe for decision-making in your life. If you are going for a vacation, do your research and settle the destination in one week. Don't allow it linger on and on and become a problem to you.

4. Start the day on a proper note

I have mentioned it before: bad mornings will most likely lead to a bad day. Take hold of your day from the morning and begin to eliminate any stressful thoughts that make want to raise their heads. You can do this by reading something that will uplift your spirit every morning, or you can practice meditation to calm your mind.

5. Understand that overthinking is bad for your mental health

Overthinking steals away all of your time and energy that should have been used for something more important. It leaves you drained and unable to achieve tangible results. By doing some of these things to your mental health, you become susceptible to anxiety and depression, which are some major triggers of suicides and suicidal thoughts.

6. Don't get too excited

Of course, people also overthink positive thoughts. For instance, you have just carried out a short survey of your business profit projection and have seen that you could get thousands of dollars richer before the year ends. You begin to imagine all the things you could do with the money, the good life you can finally have, and the things you can finally get rid of. These thoughts will consume you with baseless excitement to the extent that you might forget ideas and continue to ruminate on them over and over, basking in the beauty you imagine for yourself.

7. Document your thoughts

Get those thoughts out of your head and into a paper. It helps out sometimes. You can get a notepad close to your bed and jot down those thoughts that come to you whenever you are about to go into sleep. Once it has been put down, the brain will be forced to let go of it and free you.

8. Adopt a more carefree lifestyle

Sometimes it is best not to care. Sure, there are a lot of things that should bother you, but ask yourself how many times thinking over a situation has helped that situation. The chances are one in a million. So sometimes it is best you forget everything and live like a king. Distract yourself from your thoughts and try to practice happiness more often.

9. Get busy

The mind rarely ever has time to think when you are busy. Although it can still happen, that will only come as a form of distraction which I have taught you how to overcome. One major cause of overthinking is an unproductive mind. People who keep themselves busy hardly ever have enough time to allow them to mind wander towards baseless thoughts.

10. Realize that you can't control everything

There are things that you can control, and there are others that are simply out of your control league. You have a journey tomorrow, and the weather forecasts that it will be a rainy day. There is no need to stress yourself over it. Cancel the trip if need be and have peace of mind.

11. Purge Your Environment of overthinkers

Your environment may play a significant role in triggering overthinking. It doesn't just stop at the people close to you. It extends to the things you read, the podcasts you listen to, the trends you follow, etc. Remove all of these from your immediate environment.

12. Live in the present (not in the past or future)

The only things that should bother you are those things that are presently going on in your life. If you are in college, focus on your studies and get good grades. Prepare for the future and stop bothering about it. If you were molested as a child, find a way to forgive and move on with your life. It can be hard, but remember, it is all for you.

7 TECHNIQUES TO CONQUER THE FEAR OF FAILURE

It is natural to fear failure. Failure is never something that one would want to be associated with, and so humans shake in their boots at the sight of it. Once we are pushed outside of our comfort zone, we begin to feel that things can probably go wrong. And the truth is that failure's sting is painful and it can leave you with a blemish for the rest of your life, except if you are a person that heals quickly and moves on fast. Understand that your failures are always a springboard to your success. You might be running out of time, but that is enough reason why you should do away with the fear of failure and instead calm down. Without darkness, you will never understand light. Without cold, you will never appreciate the heat. Without failure, you will never understand the true essence of success. So, there is no need to fear failure per se. But conquering the fear of failure isn't as easy as that. You need to understand and put some things in place to fully gain the upper hand. Some of these include:

1. Understand that failing doesn't mean that you are a failure

A lot of people have failed a lot of times, but today we don't see them as failures. The examples are numerous.

- Nobody knows how many times Edison tried until he was finally able to invent the incandescent light bulb. But it is believed that it was more than a hundred times.
- An editor once told Walt Disney that his animations lacked imagination. Today, the Walt Disney company has more than fifty hugely successful animated films under its belt.
- J.K. Rowling's Harry Potter series was rejected more than ten times by different publishers until luck found her. Today she is the wealthiest author alive.

There are more examples, but the bottom line is that failure is never an endpoint except if you have decided for it to become your endpoint.

2. Learn from your failures

No matter how negative and experience is, there is always something positive to learn from it. It is only a fool that makes the same mistake twice. Sieve out all of our failures and select the benefits. They are there. You only have to look deeper and catch them. One way that can help you out is to begin to write out all the ventures that you failed in and write out the things you may have learned from failing in them.

3. View any sight of failure as a challenge to step up your game

If you think you might fail, take up the challenge, and prepare yourself not to fail. That is the only way to success. In fact, only a handful of people are totally sure of success when they first started out a venture. Most of the time, they were quite pessimistic, but they put in their best and hoped for success. Success hardly eludes people like that, except if there was a mistake made somewhere.

4. Stay optimistic and keep visualizing success

Push the thought of failure away from your mind by stay positive and thinking positivity. The thought of failing will surely come, but what if you succeed? There are two sides to this coin, and none of them should be neglected while viewing the coin. If one out of every hundred business startups in our community survives more than five years, then it could be your startup. If only one person succeeds, then it could be you.

5. Understand that the fear of failure doesn't make you a success

No matter how much you sit about achieve nothing because of failure, success will never pity you and come to your rescue. Oh, you think the fear of failure is a heavy burden to bear? Try the burden of regret and see how far that will carry you. There is nothing as painful as seeing somebody achieving the things you had always wanted to achieve, just because you allowed the fear of failure to hold you back. Shove failure off you back and make a move.

6. Be kind to yourself

If you have ever experienced failure people before, it is time to get over it. Learn from your failures and get over it. Your mind might want to keep reminding you about how bad you are, telling you that you will never be good at anything. Instead, be kind to yourself. If you made a mistake in the past, promise yourself not to go down the same part again. Then forge ahead. Nobody is ever above mistakes.

7. Avoid perfectionism

Nothing in the world is ever perfect. Every beautiful thing in the world is laced with some flaw or the other. Recognize that nothing you will ever do will be downright perfect, so go ahead and start up something. Complete the task with the mistakes and then take the time to correct the mistakes. Completing the project itself is one great step, and this will give you the urge to carry on.

6 SECRETS FOR CREATING A SUCCESS MINDSET

There can never be success without a success mindset. Those two go together like smoke and fire. There can never be one without the other. Think about most of the successful people that you know. The chance that they enter into success by mistake is pretty slim. A lot of the time, people who have a failure mindset always end up in failure, because they hardly ever identify opportunities whenever they meet them. A failure mindset will always work against you. No matter how much you try, no matter all the hard work you put in place, a mind running on failure will always produce failure. One major factor that differentiates great achievers from failures is the way they think, the content of their minds. So, to create the success you need, you need to prepare your mind for it. A failure mindset will always be shocked when success is finally achieved, but a success mindset will see success coming from a mile off. These secrets will help you develop the perfect mindset that will accommodate success:

1. Achieve small goals one at a time

When you look at your one big dream, the size of it might scare you into thinking you might fail in the long run. Remember that the large success picture does not appear at the snap of a finger. Rome was not built in a day. It was built one stone at a time. What are the stones that will build your future? Start putting them in, one block at a time. You want to win the Nobel Prize in Physics, then, you have to have a college degree in Physics first. You want to become a Pulitzer Award winner for Fiction; then, you must begin writing that novel now. These small blocks will build into one great mountain of success.

2. Take charge of your mind

We have touched little about this in Chapter 7 (taming the mind). It is easier for the mind to envision failure than to envision success. Close your eyes and imagine a plain ground, a desert without any form of life. See how easy that is to do? Now close your eyes and imagine that desert with skyscrapers, with people of all races engaging themselves in commerce. Imagine that this desert contains the tallest building in the world. See how hard it is for your mind to create a picture of wealth and abundance. If you succeeded, it must have taken you a conscious effort to do so. This is the kind of effort required to see your life as a success.

3. Be flexible and ready to tweak your plans

There is no hundred percent success plan in the world. Things can go wrong and show you the flaws in your plans. At this point, the best thing to do is to keep your mind ready for a change. It is possible that you will not achieve all the goals you attached to a plan, and that is ok. All you have to do is make sure that your mind is always ready for a change of plan.

4. You are your biggest competition

Always strive to get ahead of yourself. Know your destination and find out how fast you should move, then, move in that pace. Measuring yourself to the achievements of others can leave you with detrimental consequences. You can look up to people who have gone ahead of you and admire their lifestyle. Learn from them and keep trying to develop yourself.

5. Find a Mentor (someone that will keep you motivated)

A mentor is someone who acts like a parent to you or a master in any given field or endeavors you may find yourself. Put yourself in positions where you get to meet the best of the best in your field. Then build strong relationships with them that will turn into a mentorship. A mentor will be someone you can easily report yourself to if you make a mistake. A mentor will both scold and advise you whenever needed. And knowing that you have someone you can always look up to will provide with the needed dose of success mindset to keep you going.

6. Talk to yourself

The best advice you can get is the one you give to yourself. Sit yourself down and talk to you. Ask all the necessary questions and try to find out why things are working out the way that they are supposed to. The key here is that you have to be truthful with yourself. Take time and encourage yourself. Reward yourself. Appreciate yourself. Tell yourself you have to work harder and achieve better results. These will continually drive to achieve more at any given time.

CHAPTER 8: PLANING FOR YOUR SUCCESS

The general public does not have the same definition of success, but in a broad view, doing well in the course of action can be tagged as a success. Some are of the school of thought that success has the right outcome from a decision; a superb result after an intention is fulfilled. However you define as successful living, be sure that some elements must be seen in it. Some of them are dedication, goal setting, motivation, and problem-solving. None of these traits will be found on a path to fulfillment if you don't understand the intent behind success.

Understanding your intent gives a sense of direction. You now have a decision tool to work with. You could predict where you are coming to your destination. You may ask, "What pushes me to set those unattainable targets? Why do I envision to become muscular? "Maybe I just stumbled on it," you may reply. Ask yourself many of these questions. Comprehend what moves you. From here, the energy to keep moving towards the rough road of attainment is fueled continuously. You may not need another person to push you to fulfillment. You and the inner drive will be enough motivation to get going.

Well, success is intentional, and you could get prepared for it. That's what this chapter promises to unleash.

6 TECHNIQUES TO SUCCEED AT GOAL SETTING
1. See the birds before the sky

Don't get me wrong here. We live in a world of no limitations, and everything is possible. But you need to see the things that are closer to you first before you can reach out to things beyond. Go for a goal you can easily attain. No rule says you must start in a hard way. And you don't have to be so complicated when planning for your goals.

Achieve the little ones you can now, and the motivation will keep you inspired for the bigger ones.

2. Expand your horizon

Get your imagination to work. See yourself beyond the present level you are now. Until your inner self is motivated to achieve greatness, it will be difficult, if not impossible, to go far. Access as much information as possible to hit your goals. A better way to map out your plan is when vitality is added to the specific target.

3. Admit your setbacks

Aiming for perfection comes with loads of experience. You would not be experienced all at once in a day. What you call constant failure is what sets you on the peak. For you to move forward in fulfilling your goals, accept at every point when you fail. Acknowledging failures allows you to review your actions as well as find solutions for them. Unless you take your wrongs, you can't see the right.

4. See it the other way round

There is no cause to beat around the bush when the solution seems far. Don't get too complacent about your goal attainment. If you are stuck at an end, think of other ways to go about it. Be flexible! Sometimes, your deadline might have exceeded beyond a reasonable doubt. Get yourself going. Remember that what you want to achieve is still possible. If your goal is to study five chapters of a book in five days, and at the end of the sixth day, you are still in chapter four. Do not be discouraged and don't feel wrong about not meeting your target. Pick up the section for the next day. Ensure you review the cause of the delay and move on.

5. Be result-oriented

What should drive you is the success behind the goal. You will likely face distractions. It may come from your workplace, environment, or friends. Whatever it is, it shouldn't you stop from what you have set your mind to achieve. Think and position your brain for positivity. See every challenge as an avenue to become better. Visualize your results even before attaining them. Create a sound memory for yourself. Take pictures of what you tag as a success. Hang it around you, and let it encourage you now and then. It will not only boost your alertness; it will also make the journey to attainment fun

6. Don't get distracted

When it comes to priority, goals are not seeds of different fruits in a basket. They should be seen as fruits of a seed. Give preferences to what you want to achieve, and allow it to give birth to other goals. This approach ensures that you are orderly in your way to secure productivity. One big distraction you won't see coming is when you are trying to do many things at a time.

5 LESS-KNOWN GOAL-SETTING TIPS STRAIGHT FROM THE EXPERTS

To fetch a glass of water seems more relaxed than setting a goal sometimes. But it may seem so difficult after writing your targets, and not attaining them. It might be a long-term goal or short-term. Yours might range from career to life goals. All the same, frustration may set in when none of these look attainable. The following tips will guide you to succeed in goal setting.

1. Understand yourself

Socrates emphasized the subject of "self-knowledge." He believed that no one could be helped without self-identification. Although, major upgrades in science and technology has given a lot of answers to these worrying questions. Nonetheless, the wisdom behind getting to know the kind of human being you are is essential. It is a factor to consider for one to be successful in the course of attaining targets. Do a quick analysis of your components.

- Start by asking questions

What are you made of? Why do I think differently from others? What causes me to get anxious over little subjects? Why do I get nervous anytime I see strangers? Questions like this could not be asked until you have taken time to think of some things you often do. The aim here is not for you to feel inadequate or depressed. It is just for you to get better.

- Analyze your findings

Check your social, spiritual, health, physical, psychological, and intellectual capabilities. A game of comparison will not work here. This check is for you! What am I capable of doing? And at what pace am I capable of doing it? What makes me learn fast with little energy? "I think I sleep faster whenever I take cereals." "Oh! I doze off almost immediately whenever I rub lotion on my feet." Analyzing will give you enough reasons why you do what you do.

- Make more findings

Don't stop at your discovery. Do more research online. Find out if the traits you saw in yourself is found in other people too. How were they able to overcome it? Was it by themselves, or were they helped by a friend or professional? Is this a childhood behavior or it accompanies growing up to adulthood? Getting answers to those questions, and many more you would like to add gives you a sense of identification.

- Combine factors

You could make a temporary conclusion base on your findings. By now, you are sure that what you feel and how you feel is reasonable. Maybe what you discovered has shown to you that you need help. Good! You are making progress. Don't combine any information if you have not researched extensively. Put each of these inputs together and help yourself with it.

2.   Have a clear definition of your goal

What we sometimes see as a path can sometimes be blockage. We may tend to see possibilities at achieving a goal, but in the end, the result appears disappointing. Here is the reason. Humans have failed to properly decide without any form of prejudice what they want out of life. It is not as easy as we think, but this is what makes the goal attainment frustrating.

•   Identify the difference

Just because it is achievable does not mean it has the same strategy as other goals. Understand the difference between what is to be achieved in a short while and what is to be met for a lifetime. Define what your goal is in your terms. What someone considers as a short-term goal may be a long-term goal for you. A long-term goal cannot be achieved if it is not broken down into smaller bits. There is no technicality in this at all. A short-term goal is what you want to reach over a short period while a long-term goal will take a more extended period to attain (it can be for months or years). Your friend, who dreams of becoming a chartered accountant, may plan to go to business school for that purpose. If you are not aware that going to business school is a strategy to pursue a career goal (which is to become a chartered accountant), you might follow suit and get frustrated at the end.

•   Strategize and break down the difference

For every future, there is always a day to start it. That day is the present day you are in right now. And in a full day comprises of hours, minutes and seconds. Do a justification of what is to be done presently (at this very second) that will help the next 1,220 hours that you have set the deadline.

What you should have accomplished in the next few days should not be muddled up with next years'. You don't have to get worried over the next decade when you can successfully fulfill the project for the next day.

Your action plan might be to extract a picture of a baby and gum it at the back of your door together with an adult image. Seeing those pictures should remind you of this guide.

• Have a clear direction

This point is where decision-making is essential. Gain the confidence to know what you want. Don't forget that your composition is not only psychological. You have to be specific enough in each area of your life.

• Decide and define what you want

What do I want in life? What do I want out of life? Ask yourself those questions. Money or comfort? Some might say both. But the truth is that what we want is a comfort. And we feel that getting the kind of pleasure we want needs money to achieve it. That's true! The idea is this: We don't want our bodies to be stressed. We want our vacation to be around the cutest places around the world. The sea view apartment has always been our dream residence. Those kinds of comforts that riches can get might not sit well with some people.

Giving to orphanages gives some people relief. Donating to NGOs might give confidence to some. So, define what you want and don't get confused because of someone else's needs. Your discovery should not be stacked to your head alone. Help yourself by writing it down. Your journal or diary might be a great friend to gist with.

• Identify the process involved

Attaining a goal is not automatic. It doesn't come as we project many times. There are steps to take to be successful in it. Ensure that you maximize each process fully before going to the next. You might have set a target to read three chapters of book per day. Until you have mastered consistency in reading those three chapters, you shouldn't think of increasing your reading goals to five chapters.

- Fill the gap

Get motivated to keep going. Whenever it seems like you have missed your routine to attaining goals, get a substitute to make up for it. It might involve doing a review or progress check on your previous goals. You might decide to get more information about what you have been doing recently. Ensure that you are not lagging. Note that you are not supposed to take this as a perfect excuse for shirking responsibilities.

3. Take the first step and continue

Nothing can be as hard as having the courage to begin. Having made a proper analysis of who you are, and what you are capable of doing, you are well aware of your mental and intellectual capabilities now. It is time to put them to work.

Start with your skills. Everyone has something they are good with. And you are no exception. Commit your passion to your skills by discovering what will help you to do more. Our aim here is for you to channel those skills to ease your goal setting

4. Get a model

Imagine how a child thinks when he is writing with a pencil. It's easy at first, because his hand was held while writing. Attaining goals can be the same when there is a structure to follow.

- External model

Life is practical, so is everything that exists in it. Your big motivation might spark up from getting a life model. This model is someone who has excelled in your proposed project. You might decide to choose a leader from your workplace or in your social group. The attributes of a leader should be more inspirational than a boss. Discover one in the path of your pursuit. It might even be at your religious gathering. One of the beautiful things to discover in a model is the ready-made pattern to follow. It is more like having a template to work with. With it, life becomes more real to you. You will tend to find proper guidance on what you do.

- Be your greatest asset

It is good that there is someone around to check on us. But the biggest motivation we would get is the energy from within us. No one can encourage you more than yourself. Inspire yourself to greatness. See yourself as a helper and the one that needs help. It is a contemporary approach to solving the problem. You are both the counselor and the client. Think of the kind of advice you would give to a distressed friend. Give such to yourself when you are in distress. It might not come easy at first. Don't forget that this is your first attempt. A better way to make it go well is for you to write down crucial advice you have given before. You should be able to devise relevant admonitions that have lifted people's spirit at one time. Use them for yourself. Also, think of the congratulatory message you sent to your relative at a time when he/she did something spectacular. Say it to yourself too.

5.   Review your progress

Always have it in mind that your development is significant. Do a routine review of your goal. Ask relevant questions such as the process, the resources, sacrifice, and time involved. Don't pretend as if you have not been doing anything. Go through the first tip in this section again, and apply it to your review strategy.

7 IMPORTANT STEPS TO PLAN FOR SUCCESS

Successful living is not accidental. And to break the barrier of failed principles, you need a new awareness. Define your success, understand the purpose, and we can both work on a plan. This approach will help open up the ability to affect change in your life. It has to come as a choice for personal development.

1.   Get ready mentally

There are realities to successful living, and one of them has to start within us. You need to be prepared mentally. This means that you have settled your mind on achieving success. And being successful is the only option you have. Prepare your mind to execute a different task that will require sacrifice. There will be a reshuffle of time spent, friends to hang out with, and certain things to do at a particular period. Create that positive mindset to overcome any challenges when it surfaces. You might need to develop many skills that you are not familiar with. Be ready to embrace failure as a stepping stone to become better. Quitting should not be an escape route to failure.

2.   Maintain an expressed goal

Being specific about the kind of success you want is a better way to plan it. Express it by writing it down. You might decide to make it more professional. Structure it as a statement. Let it be as transparent as possible. Combine the right words that will set your foot running. Don't write any statement that seems too general. Let it unveil your intention to achieve results.

3.   Employ resources

It is expected that confusion will set in during the journey of success. Getting ready for such is a way to show that we are prepared for it. Seek out for influencers around you. Some people have been where you are planning to be. Discover one of them and subscribe to their teaching. Go online and sign up for emails that are relevant to your plans. Listen and follow TV shows that deal with finance and investment. Streaming several videos on YouTube wouldn't be a bad idea either.

4.   Secure a plan

By now, you should have been able to gather enough knowledge to give you an edge. Design a strategy that will most fit you. Don't forget that you don't need to generalize your methods, and starting small is something you shouldn't forget so soon. Realize the opportunities that lie in fulfilling every strategy and take it.

5.   Invest in time

By now, you should have been able to identify your priorities. Priority is very crucial in planning for success. You don't just focus on a thing without creating extra time to make it work. During this time, do more research about your plans, review them, and meditate over them. Learn what you need to know about specific action and develop yourself in it.

6.   Boosters

See and create enough motivation to keep you going. Start with your willpower. Settle every inner craving. You don't want to have setbacks again, do you? No! Then, set boosters for yourself. Don't forget that no one can give you true happiness than yourself. The same thing is real with motivation. Have reasons to find joy in your strategies to success, and that's why it is best to adopt a plan that most fits you. You may extend a bit of your motivation to your friend. This action will work well when you report your progress to them, and at every development, they reward you (based on mutual consent).

You might go the extra mile of creating what I tagged as "progress competition." It means trying to get better results at every little success. This effort will always bring consciousness to become better because you continuously see the next achievement as an upgrade to the previous. Your focus here is to ensure the consistent improvement in every course of action

7. Learn from tactics

The world revolves around ideas, and through that, innovations are born. Study world leaders and successful individuals. There are specific attributes that make them stand out in their respective fields. You may adopt some of their principles. If it performed for them, it would surely be a perfect guide for you too.

30 DAY STEP-BY-STEP PLAN TO HELP YOU BUILD HABITS AND FIRE UP YOUR PRODUCTIVITY

I believe that you have had a most amazing time going through the contents of this book. Some of the things that have listed here are small bits of the things you can do to fire up your creativity. By now you should be putting things in place to be able to conquer your distractions, create more focus and stay motivated. We know that random practices do not easily lead to success. There has to be a set-down plan to get the best out of ever set of instructions. Because of this, I have decided to gift you this 30-day step-by-step plan to enhance your creativity, motivation and productivity. This plan is loaded with small points that will change your life one day at a time for the next thirty days. All you have to do is follow it strictly and don't falter at any point, no matter how weary you may get.

This aspect of the book has been broken down into 30 parts, representing the thirty days in which the steps will be taken. You might wonder if it is really necessary to take it one day at a time. Well, it is up to you. If you have already conquered one day of the plan, you can move over to the next. Even after experiencing success, please do not forsake the instructions contained here. Go over them from time to time, probably every 60 days or as you may see fit. Take this as a guide. You know yourself best and you know how these guidelines will suit. Do not hesitate to modify them however you see fit. Don't forget to stick to every habit you are developing during these thirty days. It will change your life. I wish you success.

Day 1	Day 2
Morning	Morning
1. Exercise the body for about 10 minutes. 2. Listen to a motivating podcast. 3. Eat a well-balanced diet from the list of highly energetic foods (example: Brown rice and Sweet Potatoes). 4. Get the mind to work. Afternoon 1. Study the task at hand and try to identify the benefits open to me if I am able to complete the specific task. 2. Have a short power nap. 3. Read a book and refresh the mind.	1. Clear work desk at work. 2. Skip and exercise the body for twenty minutes. 3. Repeat some positive affirmations to myself. Afternoon 1. Try to find ways and reasons to love my job even better. 2. Break major tasks into bits. 3. Set a timeframe to complete each bit of broken-down tasks. 4. Do away with anything that may present itself as some sort of escape route from the task at hand.

Day 3	Day 4
Morning	Morning
1. Clear work desk at work.	1. Listen to a motivating podcast.
2. Skip and exercise the body for twenty minutes.	2. Clear work desk at work.
3. Repeat some positive affirmations to myself.	Afternoon
Afternoon	1. Let off a little steam doing something fun like listening to music, taking a walk with the dog, or conversing with a co-worker.
1. Study the task at hand and try to identify the benefits open to me if I am able to complete the specific task.	
2. Have a short power nap.	2. Have a short power nap if I feel tired or a little stressed out. This will help replenish my mind.
3. Read a book and refresh the mind.	
Evening	3. Try to reduce the workload at hand by pushing some to a later time.
1. Make a short assessment of my major life goals and see how far I have come towards achieving them.	Note: You are not procrastinating. You are only trying to provide your mind with the necessary clarity needed to complete a particular task.
2. Evaluate the day and scold myself of any mistakes made.	Evening
	1. Reread chapter six of this book and find out how well I have been coping with the instructions.

Day 5	Day 6
Morning	Morning
1. Creatively combine any of the energy boosting foods listed in chapter one.	1. Listen to a motivating podcast.
	2. No screen time until I complete a major task.
Afternoon	Afternoon
1. Break major tasks into bits.	4. Study the task at hand and try to identify the benefits open to me if I am able to complete the specific task.
2. Set a timeframe to complete each bit of broken-down tasks.	
3. Do away with anything that may present itself as some sort of escape route from the task at hand.	5. Have a short power nap.
	6. Read a book and refresh the mind.
	Evening
Evening	1. Evaluate the day and scold myself of any mistakes made.
1. Evaluate the day and scold myself of any mistakes made.	
2. Make important decisions for the next day this evening.	2. Go through chapter four of this book and remind yourself of its contents.

Day 7	Day 8
Morning	Morning
1. Creatively combine any of the energy boosting foods listed in chapter one.	1. Meditate for 10 straight minutes.
Afternoon	2. Clean and declutter my home and workspaces to give myself some form of clarity.
1. Take a short power nap.	
2. Eat brain fruits like blueberries.	3. Perform the most tedious task this morning.
3. Spend one hour completing a major task.	
	Evening
Evening	1. Create a list of activities for the next day.
1. Spend the evening brainstorming with people in my field who can be good mentors.	2. Read one chapter from any book.
2. Figure out practical ways in which I can connect to them and make them pick interest in helping me out.	3. Watch an inspiring video.

Day 9	Day 10
Morning	Morning
1. Listen to a motivating podcast.	1. Take a glass of water first thing this morning.
2. Creatively combine any of the energy boosting foods listed in chapter one.	2. No screen time this morning until I have completed one particular task completely.
Afternoon	Afternoon
1. Break major tasks into bits.	1. Call my mentor and talk to them about my progress.
2. Set a timeframe to complete each bit of broken-down tasks.	2. Complete one part of a major task.
3. Do away with anything that may present itself as some sort of escape route from the task at hand.	Evening
	1. Read chapter two of this book and assess how well I have followed the instructions.
Evening	2. Answer emails and reply messages.
1. Go through chapter one of this book and remind myself of its contents.	

Day 11	Day 12
Morning	Morning
1. Meditate for 15 straight minutes.	1. No screen time until 9am.
	2. Begin a major task.
Afternoon	Afternoon
1. Take a short power nap.	1. Take a short power nap.
2. Eat brain fruits like blueberries.	2. Eat brain fruits like blueberries.
3. Spend one hour completing a major task.	3. Spend one hour completing a major task.
Evening	Evening
1. List out things I am grateful for.	1. Go through chapter seven of this book and remind yourself of its contents.
2. Reward myself with something pleasurable.	2. Go to bed early for the next morning.

Day 13	Day 14
Morning	Morning
1. Creatively combine any of the energy boosting foods listed in chapter one.	1. Show gratitude for the good things in my life.
2. Call my mentor and find out how they are doing.	2. Make a short assessment of my major life goals and see how far I have come towards achieving them.
	3. Produce a clearly defined strategy for the day ahead.
Afternoon	Afternoon
1. Go for a 10-minute break and refresh the mind either with a chapter from a book or a short inspirational clip.	1. Stay conscious and try to identify the major causes of my laziness.
Evening	2. Go through chapter eight of this book and remind yourself of its contents.
1. Make a to-do list for the next day.	Evening
2. Make a list of things to be thankful for.	1. Make a to-do list for the next day.
3. Take stock of any progress made during the day.	2. Make a list of things to be thankful for.
	3. Take stock of any progress made during the day.

Day 15	Day 16
Morning 1. Listen to a motivating podcast. 2. Halfway through the 30-day plan: Assess myself and find out how well I have fared. Afternoon 1. Start an important task and timeframe for this task to be completed. 2. Take a short power nap. Evening 1. Go out and spend the night with a friend or colleague.	Morning 1. Get the mind to work by engaging in some mind games. 2. Clear work desk at work. 3. Break down all large projects into smaller ones. Afternoon 1. Take a short power nap. 2. Eat brain fruits like blueberries. 3. Spend one hour completing a major task. Evening 1. Evaluate and find out how much I have covered towards achieving my goals.

Day 17	Day 18
Morning 1. Creatively combine any of the energy boosting foods listed in chapter one. 2. No screen time until 9 AM. Use the time to finish up a major task. Afternoon 1. Go through chapter seven of this book and remind yourself of its contents. 2. Take a short power nap. 3. Eat brain fruits like blueberries. Evening 1. Go out and have fun. 2. Appreciate myself for any success recorded.	Morning 1. Creatively combine any of the energy boosting foods listed in chapter one. 2. Complete the hardest tasks of the day this morning. Afternoon 1. Try to find ways and reasons to love my job even better. 2. Break major tasks into bits. 3. Set a timeframe to complete each bit of broken-down tasks. 4. Do away with anything that may present itself as some sort of escape route from the task at hand. Evening 1. Make a short assessment of my major life goals and see how far I have come towards achieving them.

Day 19	Day 20

Morning
 	
  1. Go through chapter two of this book and remind yourself of its contents.
  2. Creatively combine any of the energy boosting foods listed in chapter one.
 	
Afternoon
 	
  1. Break major tasks into bits.
  2. Set a timeframe to complete each bit of broken-down tasks.
  3. Do away with anything that may present itself as some sort of escape route from the task at hand.
 	
Evening
 	
  1. Talk to myself and address any form of fear of failure lingering in my mind.
  2. Reaffirm some of the quotes listed in chapter three of this book.
	Morning
	
	  1. Listen to a motivating podcast.
	  2. Creatively combine any of the energy boosting foods listed in chapter one.
	
	Afternoon
	
	  1. Browse the internet and the study the lives of one successful person I admire.
	
	Evening
	
	  1. Make a list of major changes in my life since the beginning of the 30-day plan.
	  2. Reward myself.

Day 21	Day 22
Morning 　1. Creatively combine any of the energy boosting foods listed in chapter one. 　2. Start up a major task. Afternoon 　1. No screen time until 3 PM. 　2. Continue with the major task from the morning. Evening 　1. Go out and reward yourself.	Morning 　1. Listen to a motivating podcast. 　2. Meditate Afternoon 　1. Take a short power nap. 　2. Eat brain fruits like blueberries. 　3. Spend one hour completing a major task. Evening 　1. Make a short assessment of my major life goals and see how far I have come towards achieving them.

Day 23	Day 24
Morning 1. Get the mind to work by engaging in some mind games. Afternoon 1. Try to find ways and reasons to love my job even better. 2. Break major tasks into bits. 3. Set a timeframe to complete each bit of broken-down tasks. 4. Do away with anything that may present itself as some sort of escape route from the task at hand.	Morning 1. Listen to a motivating podcast. 2. Exercise for 10 minutes. Afternoon 1. Take a short power nap. 2. Eat brain fruits like blueberries. 3. Spend one hour completing a major task. Evening 1. Go out for a night with a colleague or friend.

Day 25	Day 26

Morning
  1. No screen time till 9 AM.
  2. Start on a major task.
Afternoon
  1. Study the task at hand and try to identify the benefits open to me if I am able to complete the specific task.
  2. Have a short power nap.
  3. Read a book and refresh the mind.
Evening
  1. Go through chapter six of this book and remind yourself of its contents.
  2. Complete a major task.
	Morning
	  1. Creatively combine any of the energy boosting foods listed in chapter one.
	Afternoon
	  1. Study the task at hand and try to identify the benefits open to me if I am able to complete the specific task.
	  2. Have a short power nap.
	  3. Read a book and refresh the mind.
	Evening
	  1. Make a short assessment of my major life goals and see how far I have come towards achieving them.

Day 27	Day 28

Morning
 	
  1. Creatively combine any of the energy boosting foods listed in chapter one.
  2. Assess my long-term plan and find out those that are not producing results.
  3. Brainstorm new ideas and plan to create a better solution.
 	
Afternoon
 	
  1. No screen time until I complete a major task.
  2. Task a short power nap.
  3. Go for a walk and refresh my mind.
  4. Carry out exercise four and the focus exercises listed in chapter five.
 	
Evening
 	
  1. Reward yourself for the day.
  2. Assess yourself and find out how successful you have been throughout the week.
	Morning
	
	  1. Meditate for 10 minutes.
	  4. Go through chapter eight of this book and remind yourself of its contents.
	
	Afternoon
	
	  1. Study the task at hand and try to identify the benefits open to me if I am able to complete the specific task.
	  2. Have a short power nap.
	  3. Read a book and refresh the mind.
	
	Evening
	
	  1. Make a short assessment of my major life goals and see how far I have come towards achieving them.

Day 29	Day 30
Morning	Morning
1. Creatively combine any of the energy boosting foods listed in chapter one.	1. Get the mind to work by engaging in some mind games.
Afternoon	2. Creatively combine any of the energy boosting foods listed in chapter one.
1. Go through chapter three of this book and remind yourself of its contents.	Afternoon
2. Complete a major task before having any screen time.	1. Study the task at hand and try to identify the benefits open to me if I am able to complete the specific task.
Evening	2. Have a short power nap.
1. Call my mentor and ask for advice on some specific points of concern.	3. Read a book and refresh the mind.
2. Make plans on how to implement the advice given.	Evening
	1. Make a short assessment of my major life goals and see how far I have come with achieving them.
	2. Make assessments and see how far you have come in the 30-day plan.

CONCLUSION

It has indeed been a journey, and I believe that you have been motivated to get over procrastination and fire up your productivity. But remember, doesn't end there. You have to put in your efforts to achieve success finally. It is one thing to read an excellent book and be motivated, and it is another thing to put into practice everything that has been taught. It is action that differentiates a winner from a loser. So, which will it be for yours? Will you finish this book and forget everything that was taught? I hope not, because that would be a disaster. Begin to apply all of the tactics and techniques that have been listed and see your life change for the better.

I have simplified the instructions contained in this book for you, in the form of a 30-day plan. Follow the instructions given day after day, and follow it consistently and religiously. Remember that change is a gradual process. You might not notice the change on the first day, but with time you will see that you are no longer the same person. Research has proven that any action carried out consistently for more than 21 days finally becomes a habit. So, to create the habit of productivity, you have to follow the laid-out steps I have provided you. At the end of the 30 days, you will notice a great change in your life and have a testimony share with your friends.

I wish you success and more productivity in your life as you take action today. Remember, your mind is under your control.

Printed in Great Britain
by Amazon

41629443R00066